Love and War
Between the Signs

Love and War
Between the Signs

Amy Keehn

PRIMA PUBLISHING

PRIMA PUBLISHING and its colophon are registered trademarks of Prima Communications, Inc.

Library of Congress Cataloging-in-Publication Data

Keehn, Amy.
   Love & war between the signs : astrological secrets to emotional compatability / by Amy Keehn.
     p. cm.
   Includes index.
   ISBN 0-7615-0834-1
   1. Astrology and marriage.   2. Mate selection—Miscellanea.   3. Love—Miscellanea.   I. Title.
BF1729.L6K44   1996
133.5'864677—dc20   96-26888
                                                CIP

97 98 99 00 HH 10 9 8 7 6 5 4
Printed in the United States of America

How to Order

Single copies may be ordered from Prima Publishing, P.O. Box 1260, Rocklin, CA 95677; telephone (916) 632-4400. Quantity discounts are also available. On your letterhead, include information concerning the intended use of the books and the number of books you wish to purchase.

Visit us online at http://www.primapublishing.com

Dedication

I dedicate this book to women everywhere who have struggled desperately to salvage relationships with men whom they loved very dearly, but who were simply not on their emotional wavelength. These were men who could never really understand how these women felt—men with whom they could never develop true emotional intimacy—men with whom they were astrologically incompatible!

Contents

Foreword
Acknowledgments
Introduction
Author's Note
Basic Information About Astrology
The Emotional Elements
The Mental Elements

HOW TO "KNOW" A MAN
YOU DO NOT KNOW

THE EMOTIONAL *VERSUS* THE MENTAL ELEMENTS

Fire and Water People: Feeling Has Priority

12. The Feeling Sign Men: Fire and Water 135

Earth and Air People: Thinking Has Priority

13. Thinking Sign Women: Earth and Air 159

14. Thinking Sign Men: Earth and Air 187

SOME FINAL THOUGHTS

Foreword

L*ove and* War Between the Signs offers an astrological explanation of the theories on which I based my book, *Men Are from
Mars, Women Are from Venus.* My awareness of men and women
having both Martian and Venusian characteristics was directly
influenced by my knowledge of the ancient practice of astrology. This was a result of my mother's intense interest in this
subject. I knew that being male or female was not the only factor determining one's needs and actions. I came to realize that
we have to take into consideration the effect of astrology and
the influence of all twelve Signs.

Amy Keehn explores this issue with great insight and humor,
providing us with a fascinating look at astrological compatibility that will help enlighten the world as to why chart influences
are so important in understanding a mate's innate behavior patterns. She delves into an issue that I have often written about—
that of role reversal—offering suggestions as to how men and
women can develop both sides of their nature.

Amy looks at the problems that ensue when people are unable to balance gender energies—for example, men with too
many planets in the Martian signs of Air and Fire being "Super-
Martians" in their approach to relationships. Also discussed is
the opposite imbalance: women who have too many planets
in the "Venusian Signs" of Water and Earth. There can be very
real problems which I have frequently referred to: caring too
much, doing too much, worrying too much about everyone
but themselves. Of course, there are those who have the good

fortune to be born with a balance of Martian and Venusian qualities.

The essence of this thought-provoking book pertains to what I wrote about in *Men, Women, and Relationships,* wherein I talked about the "emotional person" judging an "analytical person" as "too analytical," while the "analytical person" judges the "emotional person" as "too emotional." Amy offers the astrological reasons for this difference in approach, explaining how an individual's more mental or more emotional nature is determined by the Element of their Sun Sign.

You will be intrigued by a number of other astrological theories pertaining to relationship compatibility. These are examined in a manner which, like the rest of the book, is easily understood by all.

John Gray, Ph.D

Acknowledgments

A million thanks to author and friend Naura Hayden for her continuing encouragement and her enthusiastic support of *Love and War Between the Signs.*

An enormous debt of gratitude to my sister and best friend, Carol Panian. With Sun, Mars, Mercury, and Ascendant in Capricorn, one can only imagine how invaluable her input was in editing, re-editing, and re-editing.

Introduction

The divorce rate in this country has reached tragic propor-
tions. The very fabric of our society is being profoundly affected.
Certainly there are many factors involved when marriages fail,
ranging from financial pressures to the emotional maturity levels
of the individuals. But what about couples who just do not seem
to understand each other emotionally? Might the issue of astrological incompatibility play a part in the downfall of marriages
that initially seem promising? Are there couples who really are
hopelessly emotionally mismatched? If so, is there a way to
easily determine whether a given couple can ever meet each
other's emotional needs effectively enough to have a healthy
relationship?

In recent years, there has been a growing trend toward using
the 6,000-year-old science of astrology as a tool to help people
understand and overcome their problems. As an astrological
therapist specializing in couple compatibility, I have repeat-
edly seen couples who were complete emotional opposites. I
am not referring to personality differences; it is not always a
problem when one party is more introverted and the other is
more outgoing. I am referring to men and women who could
not even comprehend the basic emotional nature of their
mates, and thereby were unable to respond in a meaningful
way. Many of these couples, though they loved each other
deeply, simply could not overcome the fact that they were so
different emotionally.

It was not always women who were the emotional ones,
complaining that their husbands did not want to talk about
their feelings. It was often the other way around. There were
many men who felt that their wives or girlfriends were not

comfortable expressing their feelings or experiencing too much emotion, and indeed their mates described these men as being too emotionally intense or needy.

I began searching for common denominators in the charts of those who were innately in need of frequent emotional feedback, and of those who were actually made uncomfortable by this type of emotional interaction. I found myself referring to the two distinctly different types of people as Feelers and Thinkers even prior to discovering the astrological key to these profoundly different types of individuals. I discovered that it came down to a clash of the Thinking and Feeling Elements of their Sun Signs—"a war between the Signs!" In order for couples to relate and respond to each other's emotional needs, they must both have either Mental or Emotional Sun Signs, making them both Thinkers or both Feelers.

The Emotional Element Sun Sign person wants and needs to feel strongly emotionally connected. The Mental Element Sun Sign person is actually made anxious by this level of emotional connection and has a distinct need to feel more emotionally independent.

If your Sun Sign is associated with an Emotional Element (Water: Cancer, Scorpio, or Pisces; or Fire: Aries, Leo, or Sagittarius), you will relate best to men of these Signs who are prone to feeling first, then thinking. They are inclined to base their decisions on how they feel, and have a greater need for their mates to be emotionally responsive. If the men you have been involved with have found you too emotional, and have made you feel that you needed too much emotional intimacy, then they were probably Mental Sun-Sign men (Earth or Air Sun Signs).

The opposite will be the case if your Sign is associated with one of the Mental Elements (Earth: Taurus, Virgo, or Capricorn; or Air: Gemini, Libra, or Aquarius). You will find that the only men who are truly on your emotional wavelength will be the men of these Signs. Like you, they will tend to think first and then feel. They are inclined to base their decisions on what they think, and they will not relate well to constant emotional interaction. These men will appreciate your being somewhat emotionally reserved. However, if you tend to find yourself defending your need for emotional independence and privacy, and you are tired of men who seem to be emotionally needy, then you have probably been dating men who are Emotional Sun Signs (Fire or Water).

Although you may be eager to read about your Sign, please resist the temptation to do so until you read Chapter 3: The Clash Between Thinkers and Feelers. Then, when you read about your Sign, it will be easier to understand why you are so emotionally incompatible with certain Signs of the zodiac.

Also, when reading about your Sign, don't skip the basic information on your Element. For instance, if you are a Leo, be sure to read "The Fire Sign Women" in Chapter 11, as the issues discussed therein pertain to women of all three Fire Signs.

After you have determined whether his Sun Sign is a matching Element for you, you will want to explore the *Martian/ Venusian* influences in his chart. This all-important issue of gender balance will indicate his capability to communicate in a normal and balanced way. Dr. John Gray's number-one bestselling book *Men Are from Mars, Women Are from Venus* makes the terms *Martian* and *Venusian* so widely accepted that I will be using them frequently in this book. Chapter 5: Why Can't a Man Be More Like a Woman? explains why some men are *Super-Martians,* while others let the world walk all over them (these men are from Venus). The Elements of Air and Fire are masculine, and the men who want to take charge and rule the world have a major influence in these Elements. The chronically passive individual has too many planets in the feminine Elements of Water and Earth. Of course, these chart influences affect women as well. Chapter 5 also details the importance of learning to blend the Martian and Venusian energies to become what Dr. Gray describes as *Marusian.*

In Chapter 6: The Male Chauvinist, Astrologically Defined, I will go into greater depth on this crucial gender issue by explaining how males with too much masculine influence (too many planets in the Air or Fire Signs) simply have more masculine energy than they know what to do with. Such a chart produces a classic type of "Mr. Wrong"—the male chauvinist.

These are the Super-Martians, whose lack of the feminine Elements of Earth and Water leaves them at a disadvantage when it comes to understanding, much less meeting, the needs of a Feeling woman.

Perhaps the "man of your dreams" has turned out to be your worst nightmare because he has not reached emotional maturity. After reading Chapter 7: Is He an Emotional Grownup?, you will probably have a renewed belief in the importance of a man being able to approach life's challenges from an emotionally centered space. You want a man with emotional intelligence.

You will not want to miss Chapter 8: Men Who Are Hopelessly Self-Centered. A glance at a man's chart will tell you whether he is capable of caring about you as much as he cares about himself. This chapter also explains the chart factor that makes a man codependent—caring "too much" and smothering you with his affection.

Incidentally, the Element of a man's Sun Sign is extremely important as a starting point for emotional compatibility, but it is only a starting point. By knowing his exact date of birth, you will be able to determine the Element influence of all of his planets. There is simply no other way to "know" a man you don't know. Wouldn't it be helpful to know that the man you might let into your heart is actually someone you would rather not let into your garage sale?

Some day you will be glad that you persevered until you found Mr. Right for You. Never settle for anything less than a man whose Sign is "at peace" not "at war" with yours—and a man who is an emotional grownup! There really is a man out there who will not only be on your emotional wavelength, but will be as considerate as your best friend and care as much about you as your mother. You just have to find him (see Chapter 18: "Somewhere Out There").

Author's Note

I must clarify a misconception that may occur when people first learn that the Feeling Signs of Water and Fire are much more emotionally oriented than the mental Thinking Signs of Earth and Air. You may think of people you know—Thinkers who seem very emotional, and Feelers who do not; however, the differences between these Elements do not pertain to personality, but rather to the fundamental emotional make up of the individual and how comfortable he or she feels when coping with emotional issues and expressing feelings. (Ironically, Thinking Sign individuals are often very emotional about not being more comfortable with emotion.)

While couples must be of the same Sign Type—both Thinkers or both Feelers—in order to have any real potential for emotional intimacy and "relationship flow," there is even greater emotional rapport between individuals of the same exact Element.

The Two Emotional Elements—The Feelers

Fire people, the most romantic of the Zodiac, share a unique brand of passion and emotional intensity.

The Water Sign couple experiences a level of ultra-emotional sensitivity that is unknown to the other Elements.

The Two Mental Elements—The Thinkers

Earth individuals' practical nature produces a down-to-earth and "realistic" approach to life and love. The Air couple will share an abstract, futuristic brand of thinking and can relate to one anothers' need for "emotional space."

Chapter 4: The Matches and the Mismatches provides a succinct overview of the emotional natures of these four Elements, as well as the crucially important part that the differences between them play in our relationships. This chapter captures the essence of the emotional rapport—or lack thereof—between two Elements.

Basic Information About Astrology

What Is an Astrological Chart?

Your natal chart could be thought of as a "map" of the sky showing the exact location of the planets and which Signs they were in at the moment of your birth.

What Is an Element?

In the science of astrology, each Sign is associated with one of the four Elements of the universe: Earth, Air, Water, or Fire. There are three Earth Signs, three Air Signs, three Water Signs, and three Fire Signs. One's entire approach to life and love is profoundly affected by the Element associated with one's Sun Sign. For instance, the behavior of someone whose Sun is located in any of the three Water Signs will reflect the sensitive, loving qualities and traits attributed to this Element.

This book is based on the very different emotional needs of the Mental Elements of Earth and Air and the Emotional Elements of Water and Fire.

What Is a Mode?

A Mode is the channel through which an Element functions. There are three Modes: Cardinal (ambitious), Fixed (determined), and Mutable (flexible). This explains why Mutable

Virgo men are more easygoing and flexible than the more stubborn Fixed Taurus men.

Major Planets

These are the planets that have the greatest overall affect on who we are, from our basic values and character to our emotional nature (Sun, Moon, Mercury, Venus, Mars, Ascendant).

Functional Planets

This term refers to the three planets that seem to most determine how we function in life: Mercury (how we think), Venus (how we love), and Mars (how we act).

Astrological Explanation for "Martian" and "Venusian"

Why do some men seem to come from Venus while others are Super-Martians? This is determined by the distribution of Elements in their astrological charts. Fire and Air Signs are masculine or "Martian" and Earth and Water signs are feminine or "Venusian." It is the number of masculine Elements versus feminine Elements in a man's chart that indicates just how "Martian" he will be.

The Emotional Elements
The Feeling Signs

Water and Fire Signs need to *feel* their emotions and express them. They tend to *feel* first, and then *think,* and are prone to basing their decisions on how they *feel.*

Water Signs

CANCER (June 21–July 23)
SCORPIO (October 23–November 22)
PISCES (February 19–March 20)

Water Sign Qualities

Gentle, Kind, Sensitive, Sympathetic, Understanding, Forgiving, Compassionate

Fire Signs

ARIES (March 20–April 20)
LEO (July 23–August 23)
SAGITTARIUS (November 22–December 21)

Fire Sign Qualities

Confident, Enthusiastic, Dynamic, Passionate, Idealistic, Futuristic, Confrontive

The Mental Elements
The Thinking Signs

Earth and Air Signs are less comfortable feeling their emotions and expressing them. They tend to *think* first, and then *feel,* and are prone to basing their decisions on what they *think.*

Earth Signs

TAURUS (April 20–May 21)
VIRGO (August 23–September 23)
CAPRICORN (December 21–January 19)

Earth Sign Qualities

Practical, Down to Earth, Realistic, Responsible,
Cautious, Conventional

Air Signs

GEMINI (May 21–June 21)
LIBRA (September 23–October 23)
AQUARIUS (January 20–February 19)

Air Sign Qualities

Intellectual, Abstract, Analytical, Imaginative,
Restless, Romantic, Truthful, Curious

How to "Know" a Man You Do Not Know

1

The End

Hallelujah! You have reached the end—the end of "relationship blindness!" It will now be possible to see into the soul and mind of a man before you make a commitment (or before you *are* committed)! You hold in your hands a guide to recognizing Mr. Right—a ray of light in what may have heretofore been a depressing wasteland of astrologically disastrous relationships. Isn't it about time that you had a simple way of distinguishing a potential Mr. Right from an almost certain Mr. Wrong? Why spend the next decade of your life attempting to have meaningful emotional interaction with men who are clueless, and who view your emotional needs with disdain?

Welcome to a new realm of insight into what may have been a world of agonizing attempts to understand how the man—who you mistakenly perceived as the love of your life—could possibly have done what he did or said what he said—or perhaps even worse, not have done or said the truly obvious! At best, dating may have consisted of haphazard coupling that has landed you in more than one semi-compatible or barely tolerable situation. Never again!

You Can't Fix Mr. Wrong

Perhaps the problem is not so much an inability to recognize Mr. Wrong as it is the tendency to remain in relationships while

3

trying to fix the unfixable. This book is about not getting into these emotionally unworkable situations in the first place. Won't that be a time-saver? Unfortunately, many women seem to have a strong urge to hang on to men who continually prove themselves unworthy of another hour of their time. This may come from our motherly nurture-and-rescue instinct, or from the debilitating "any port in a storm" syndrome. Both produce the same result: a waste of precious time and emotions. The idea is to find a man with whom you can grow old, not to grow old finding him!

You obviously will not have time to find the right man if you are staying in a relationship with the wrong man. The key is to not get involved with the wrong man in the first place. With the help of this book, you will now be able to readily know whether a man is on your emotional wavelength. You will be able to avoid dating a man who, in the past, you might have married—a man who might have cost you years and sapped the loving energies right out of you. And then what happens? Forget loving a man, you may no longer love yourself!

Is it any wonder that you've been going crazy, fighting an up-hill battle in attempting to communicate emotionally with men who seemed to be on another planet? You can now relax in the knowledge that there is hope! You may have just been inter-acting with men of the wrong Signs—men who were not on your emotional planet.

Avoiding the War Between the Signs

Half of the Signs of the zodiac are on such a different emotional wavelength from you that I have come to refer to this clash as "the war between the Signs."

After you read Chapter 3: The Clash Between Thinkers and Feelers, you will wonder how you ever muddled through the dating maze without this vital information. By knowing only a man's Sun Sign, you will be able to determine whether there is any point in pursuing things further. You will know whether this man is someone with whom you could potentially feel emotionally comfortable.

You will become a believer in the importance of knowing a man's astrological chart before you become involved. During that deceptive little game called "courtship behavior," a man can hide anything—from having the maturity level of a first-grader to sociopathic tendencies—behind a mask of thoughtful remarks, charm, and humor! But his planet placements will easily give you many crucial pieces of information. Does his chart indicate that he is exceptionally self-centered, with a powerful need to manipulate and control others? Or does it show that he is capable of genuinely caring about and responding to the needs of another?

Imbalances in a man's chart can produce an individual with serious problems. The chart can indicate a multitude of ego malfunctions, ranging from general impatience with a world that doesn't respond to his every need, to a spoiled-child attitude when he is confronted with proof of this fact. Without the advantage of astrological knowledge, it may take weeks or even months to know what you could have known about a man in five minutes.

If you are determined to pursue a man whose chart has real problem areas, at least you can be on the lookout for the first signs of abnormal behavior, rather than being caught off guard when he shows his true colors. I can hear you now: "But he is so wonderful and seems so sensitive that I just have to give him a chance." It may take some time for you to become a true believer in this science, but you will eventually get to the point where you will no longer be willing to enter into a relationship with someone whose emotional needs differ greatly from your own or whose chart indicates major imbalances.

In retrospect, I am sure you will agree that, in some cases, you may have been more discriminating in the selection of a feline or canine companion. After all, your pet will share your life, if not your bed, love you with undying loyalty, watch TV by the fire with you on many cold lonely nights, greet you after a long absence with enthusiastic kisses about the face and neck, and stare intently into your eyes to let you know that he is there for you when you are sad or forlorn—actually, not entirely unlike a man! Take heart! You now have guidelines—a checklist that will be of great assistance in determining just how any given gentleman under consideration will match up to your trusty spaniel or Lhasa Apso in the aforementioned areas! After all, a man requires a bit more of your vital life force than just a comfortable bed, a well-balanced diet, and regular trips to the doctor for an update on shots. The time to find out just how trustworthy this creature is, is before you invest—not just your time and your money, but your heart savings! Read on and learn more about how it is truly possible to put an end to "blind" dating!

2

When a Man Is Not True . . . to His Sign!

Is it possible? An Aries man who is not Mr. "Let Me Show You How That Should Be Done"? Is there such a thing as a Gemini man who does not have to be in control of everything? Believe it or not, it is possible! People are not always typical examples of their Sun Signs. When is a Taurus not so bullish? When his Mercury is in Gemini, adding flexibility and perspective to his thinking process, and when he expresses affection like a Cancer because his Venus is in this gentle Water Sign.

There are planet placements that can cause a person to demonstrate behavior not in keeping with the basic nature of their Sun Sign. You may find a Virgo who does not have to iron his socks, or perhaps a Leo who does not thrive on center stage. The Virgo in question could have major planets in Sagittarius and Gemini, and would be too disorganized to *find* his socks, much less iron them. And as for our shy Leo, who is extremely un-lion-like; he might have the planets of Mercury, Venus, and Mars in the Water Sign of Cancer. How Leo could he appear to be when he thought (Mercury), loved (Venus), and acted (Mars) like a Cancer? However, even with no other planets in Leo or the other Fire Signs, he would be still very much a Leo in terms of his basic sense of self, his values, and

7

his fundamental emotional wavelength. The Sun Sign alone determines one's basic emotional nature.

The Function of the Planets

As you read the following descriptions of each planet's function, you will gain a better understanding of the complexity of human nature. Note that the planets will not line up again in the same position they were in on your birth date for another 25,000 years! Even though the placement of all the major planets is important in making every human being unique, your Sun Sign is of singular importance in the area of emotional style. This may seem ironic, because the Sign of Venus in our chart governs how we relate to love. But regardless of other planet placements, the effect of the Sun Sign on people's emotional patterns is so enormous that nothing alters the tremendous difference in the emotional needs of the clashing Sun Signs.

Sun

When people ask you what "Sign" you are, they are referring to the Sign (the section of the sky) the Sun was in at the time when you were born. The traits and urges of your Sun Sign will indeed be a big part of who you are—your basic sense of self, your values and psychological bias. But you may or may not be a typical example of that Sign. This will depend largely upon how many of the other planets are also be in the same Sign or Element as your Sun, and whether important planets are located in Signs that have very different qualities than your Sun Sign. When your Sun Sign is in an emotional Element (the Feeling Signs of Fire or Water), you will basically be comfortable with feeling and expressing emotion. When your Sun Sign is in a Mental Element (the Thinking Signs of Earth and Air), you will basically be uncomfortable with too much display of emotion. Hence, the war between the Signs!

Moon

The needs and desires associated with the Sign in which your Moon is located will tell you about the deepest emotional part of you (second in importance only to your Sun Sign). Your Moon placement rules your habits and moods—all that is emotionally instinctive and subconscious. A man whose Sun Sign is Cancer is a real homebody, but if his Moon is in Aries, he will be an adventurer at heart as well. He'll be more adventurous than the typical Cancer, probably displaying this tendency even more after the age of 30, when one is more inclined to act from the needs of one's Moon. Also, when we become upset, we react from the instincts of the Element of our Moon.

I think that the worst Element for a man's Moon is Earth. Because we function through the Element of our Moon when we are emotional, and because Earth is the most unemotional of the Elements, it can be a difficult placement. At the very time when you want him to be the most emotionally expressive— when he is feeling emotional—this man is inclined to sound like a news update. While other factors in the chart enter into the picture, frequently those with an Earth Moon will seem unable to "speak emotion" in a manner that makes you feel it. You're hearing logic and practicality (Earth) when you are yearning to hear how he *feels!*

Mercury

The planet of communication, Mercury is the brain of the chart; it determines how you think and how you communicate your thoughts. The placement of this planet tells us whether people, when thinking about a specific issue, will be more practical and reasonable or more emotional in their conclusions. The traits of the Sign of Mercury in your chart will influence your thinking patterns. Mercury pertains to how you perceive the world around you and how you relay those perceptions. Naturally, when Mercury is found in either of the Thinking Elements—the Earth or Air Signs—there is a more logical or rational approach to thinking. However, when Mercury is found in an Emotional Element—one of the Water or Fire Signs)—an individual's thinking can be colored by emotions, interfering with the clarity of the reasoning process. Does this sound familiar? I'll bet that we have all known a few men with an emotional Mercury in a Water or Fire Sign. It matters not that you may think he is a reasonable Virgo gentleman; if his Mercury is in the emotional Fire Sign of Leo, you can forget all about common sense and logic if the issue he is trying to sort out is extremely emotional in nature. A man whose Sun Sign is Pisces, with the gentle flexible ways of this Mutable Sign, can show all the stubbornness of Taurus the Bull if he has Mercury (the brain of his chart) in the Fixed and stubborn Sign of Taurus.

Venus

Venus is the planet of love and beauty. We approach love and affection (not just romantic love), with the hopes, dreams, and desires associated with the Sign in which Venus is located in our chart. These are the needs that we bring to a relationship regarding love. This Sign determines how we express love, how we need to have love expressed to us, and how we relate to partnership and mutual giving. Since the planet Venus has such a strong influence on a man's behavior within a love relationship, let us review the effect that Venus has in each of the four Elements.

Fire Venus

Many individuals with a Fire Venus are too demanding and perfectionistic; they tend to pout when you do not read their minds. Love must be exciting for Fire Venus people; they need (and are capable of) the grand romantic gestures.

A Fire Venus can cause difficulties for a man who is not even a Fire Sun Sign (see Chapter 6: The Male Chauvinist, Astrologically Defined). There tends to be a common problem with any Fire Venus individual (male or female) when it comes to basic communication skills. They can have great difficulty in understanding or even respecting the values, actions, and decisions of a person whose approach or reaction to a situation is different from theirs. Not only may they be unable to relate to the other person's feelings or response to the issue, but they often proceed to inform them of this in an intense, opinionated fashion! Almost invariably, they are very judgmental about the whole matter. They may then proceed to tell you exactly how you should have felt, reacted to, and handled the situation.

Water Venus

When we find Venus in the kind, loving Element of Water, it produces a man who, regardless of his Sun Sign, tends to express affection in a gentle and loving manner. He will need a partner who is very kind and thoughtful. Unfortunately, a man or woman with a Water Venus is invariably far too concerned with the feelings of others. They so hate to hurt anyone that they may remain in a negative situation forever because of their inability to cause the other person pain or rejection. This is also due to Water's nonconfrontive nature.

It would be wonderful if Water Venus people understood that, in order to build true emotional intimacy with someone, they must be honest with them. By not letting you know how he really feels, a man is in essence "lying" to you. But he does not want to upset you by being critical of you. This is the man who will finally tell you, after you've worn your hair for ten years in a way that you thought he liked, that he never really cared for it!

Air Venus

An Air Venus has a very idealistic, romantic view of love— poetry and candlelight! He has a charming and refreshing way of letting candid remarks fall out of his mouth. As with an

Earth Venus, he will have a more mental approach to romance, but it will be of the analytical variety.

There are some problem areas common to Air Venus men. Air is idealistic and perfectionistic, and this man can demonstrate a real need to be in control of his romantic endeavors. With Air being highly sensitive, those with this Venus placement can be very touchy when it comes to getting their feelings hurt. He will either give you the typical Air "distant and removed" treatment, or, since Air is a confrontive Element, he might decide to let you know how he feels. At times he can also display a cold, distracted quality so common to the Element of Air. He can suddenly distance himself from you emotionally as he relates to you from that distracted Venus in an Air Sign. A simple, slightly insensitive remark could be enough to trigger this response.

Earth Venus

In the passion department, Earth is second only to Fire, (Earth being the most sensuous Element). There is something refreshing about a man who can approach love without being overly perfectionistic (Fire Venus), ultrasensitive (Water Venus), or aloof (Air Venus). However, Earth Venus people very much need tangible commitment! They don't want to wonder how you feel; they need to know where you stand.

Mars

Mars governs how we act, how we go forth in the world—action without specific thought or feeling. Mars is your method of operation: how you function; the manner in which you handle, manage, and organize your work, activities, hobbies, and so on. Mars also pertains to aggression. A down-to-earth Taurus man with Mars in the Air Sign of Gemini would have a restless impatience about him. A very fiery Aries man would benefit from Mars in the Water Sign of Pisces, adding gentleness and a more thoughtful, flexible manner.

The Outer Planets

The influence of the outer planets is of less importance than the major planets. However, the placement of each of the outer planets has a specific effect in the area of life that it governs, and ultimately defines the absolute uniqueness of the individual. These planets can have a very important affect on a chart in terms of how they aspect (contact) the major planets.

Jupiter

Jupiter governs our basic attitude and disposition toward others—our inner spirit that motivates our feelings and general behavior toward the world. Are we warm and generous, or cold and serious, in the way we reach out to others? Does a person reach out in a kind and nurturing manner (Jupiter in Cancer), or in a cautious and practical manner (Jupiter in Capricorn)? The placement of Jupiter indicates our enthusiasm and symbolizes how we will receive new ideas and information, how we expand our consciousness, and how we learn and grow. When Jupiter aspects another planet in your chart, it will add a generous, benevolent quality to the specific functions pertaining to that planet. For instance, when Jupiter is in the same Sign as Venus in a chart, it will add a generosity of spirit and a happy, positive attitude to one's approach to love.

Saturn

Saturn is the planet of discipline, restriction, limitation, caution, and restraint. You gain a sense of yourself by mastering the shortcomings of the Sign of your Saturn; ego problems can be found by examining the placement of Saturn in your chart. If an individual has difficulty accepting, or even acknowledging, their part in relationship problems, it may be tied in with their Saturn. Also, one must meet the needs of the Sign of their Saturn in order to feel safe. When Saturn aspects another planet in your chart, it will tend to restrict or discipline the functions pertaining to that planet.

Uranus

Uranus is the planet of flash insight, originality, and intuition. The placement of Uranus tells us how individualistic a person is. It tells us how much independence and freedom this person requires. This planet also pertains to erratic actions—acting without rhyme or reason, sudden changes, and spontaneous behavior. Uranus can really wreak havoc with a person when it contacts a planet such as Venus, causing impulsiveness or erratic behavior in the way one approaches love and relationships. When it contacts Mercury (the brain of the chart), it makes for a highly original and quick thinking process. Uranus aspecting any planet in a chart adds an independent, impulsive energy to the specific functions pertaining to that planet.

Neptune

Neptune rules the Sign of Pisces and can cause confusion, illusion, and delusion. Those with a strong Neptune emphasis in their charts seem to live in a fantasy world of their own making. Inspirational and mystical, Neptune relates to the deepest wells of the subconscious—what we wish and hope to become, our secret yearning or image of our lives. When Neptune aspects another planet in your chart, its effect will be to cloud or confuse the functions pertaining to that planet.

Pluto

Pluto is the planet of obsession and compulsion, of extremes and radical action. The female lead character, played by Glenn Close, in *Fatal Attraction* is an illustration of what can happen when a Pluto aspect to Venus runs amuck. But there is also a rejuvenation factor about Pluto; it can destroy suddenly, then teach you to rebuild with creative freedom to make a fresh start while remembering the mistakes of the past. When Pluto contacts another planet in your chart, it will produce obsessive, compulsive urges regarding the functions pertaining to that planet.

The Ascendant or Rising Sign

Personal style and mannerisms, as well as the way in which an individual approaches new projects in life, is also governed by one's Ascendant. The Ascendant can be determined by knowing the exact time of birth—it is the zodiac Sign rising on the horizon at the time of your birth. This may or may not coincide with your inner personality, but it is the way in which others perceive you. For instance, an Ascendant in a Water Sign or Fire Sign will add an emotional quality to the personality and could make a Thinking Sign appear to be more of a Feeling Sign. This can be very deceptive. He is still a Thinker who will never meet the emotional needs of a Feeling Sign woman.

3

The Clash Between
Thinkers and Feelers

There is not so much a war between the *sexes* as there is a war between the *Signs*. Half of the zodiac clashes emotionally with the other half. A couple whose Signs clash may spend their lives trying to come to terms with this emotional gap in their relationship. Let's look at such a couple.

Michael, a Libra, and Shelby, a Leo, have been dating for three years. Shelby believes that she loves Michael, but she is bothered that she doesn't really "feel" his love for her, even though she *knows* he does really love her. But he is a terrific guy—mature, funny, bright, and kind.

Michael is over an hour late, and has not called. That's not like him. Shelby is worried and upset. Michael finally arrives, but does not acknowledge her feelings. He just tells her there is nothing to be upset about. His reason for not calling? He just received his cell-phone bill—no more nonessential calls.

During dinner Shelby describes an incident at work that day involving a co-worker making a highly inappropriate comment about her in front of the boss. Michael replies that she doesn't need to be so emotional about it. Her boss certainly knows how indispensable she is to the company and must have disregarded such a remark.

Later in the evening, they discuss their relationship. Shelby would like a commitment—after all, they have been dating for three years. Michael responds, "I think I need to take some time to evaluate all the aspects of this situation before I make a decision. You know I've been preoccupied with work lately." Shelby asks, "What do you love about me?" He answers, "You're intelligent, mature, communicative, and responsible." Her view of herself is different; she feels that she is dynamic, creative, funny, passionate, and devoted. She wonders if he truly loves her.

The obvious differences between Michael and Shelby are not just a result of his being a "right-brain male" and her being an "emotional female"! Their Air and Fire Sun Signs are at war emotionally. Michael's Air Sign (Libra) approaches emotion with rational thinking and caution; he considers all factors before deciding how he feels. He is wary of feelings that cannot be thoroughly analyzed and controlled. He cherishes his emotional independence and doesn't relate to talking much about his feelings with his mate. On the other hand, Shelby's Fire Sign (Leo) approaches emotion with eagerness and enthusiasm, arriving at decisions by following her heart and her instincts. She thrives on emotional interaction and feeling emotionally connected to her mate.

This couple provides a classic illustration of how far apart people are emotionally when there is a clash of Signs—when their Signs are on different emotional wavelengths.

Why are people of certain Signs so incredibly different in terms of what we will call their "emotional profile" (how comfortable one is with emotion, how one copes with emotional issues, whether one relates in a positive way to emotion or is fearful of too much feeling)?

The explanation is really very simple. Of the four Elements—Fire, Water, Earth, and Air—two Elements differ drastically from the other two in terms of their emotional make-up. Two of these Elements virtually thrive on emotion, while the other two are wary of emotion.

A person's emotional profile is determined by whether the Element of his or her Sun Sign is Mental or Emotional. Those with Mental Sun Signs (Earth and Air) are the "Thinkers," and those with Emotional Sun Signs (Water and Fire) are the "Feelers."

This gives us two extraordinarily different types of people. There is such a tremendous difference in the way these two types function emotionally that it is imperative that your efforts at building emotional intimacy be with someone of the same emotional type—someone who is emotionally compatible.

If your Sun Sign is one of the Thinking Elements, you operate on a more mental level, reacting to situations in terms of what you think. The Thinker's response to life is fundamentally a more mental one: thinking first and then feeling. There is a tendency to give thoughts and facts priority over feelings. If your Sun Sign is one of the Feeling Elements, you operate on a more emotional level, reacting to things in terms of how you feel. The Feeler's response to life is innately emotional: feeling first and then thinking. These individuals tend to give their feelings priority over thoughts and facts.

Thinkers find it difficult to cope with emotions. Feelers operate in a completely different manner. This is not to say that they like unpleasant feelings or emotional scenes, but that they are simply able to process feelings with greater ease. Feeling emotions is more natural to them; they seem to take to feeling as a fish does to water. On the other hand, a Thinker who is confronted with too much emotion is more like a cat in a swimming pool; it is uncommon to find one who tolerates the water very well, and very rare indeed to find one who actually likes to swim.

Think of it as similar to needing a partner with a compatible sense of humor—who laughs at the same silly, crazy, or irreverent things that amuse you. If you have a great sense of the ridiculous, there is little more annoying than to be falling on the floor with mirth, unable to catch your breath, as the man of your dreams sits there staring at you, wondering whether a state facility would provide adequate care. You need a man who responds to emotionality in the same way you do. Otherwise he might be wondering the same thing when you are expressing emotion in a manner that is normal for you, but which for him translates into "emotional basket case."

The basic contrast between the nature of the Thinkers and the Feelers is extremely pronounced, making them almost as different from one another as men are from women. Given the innate emotional differences between the sexes, you can see the importance of having the man in your life be of an emotionally compatible Sun Sign. Without this factor in your favor, it would be extremely difficult to achieve any level of true emotional intimacy.

Emotional Sign people have trunks full of "emotional toys" that they want to share with you. They would like to throw them all over the room and roll around in them. But the Thinking Sign people will want to keep their emotional toys in a display case, taking them out (when they're in the mood, and when they're in control) to carefully look at and enjoy them in a more civilized fashion. The bottom line is that there is nothing wrong with either approach. The goal is simply not to have two people with such opposite attitudes about emotion sharing the same intimate relationship.

The Thinking Signs

The Earth Signs: Capricorn, Taurus, Virgo

A more practical, down-to-earth brand of thinking: Logical, Detail-minded, Realistic, Conventional, Cautious.

* * * * * * * *

The Air Signs: Aquarius, Gemini, Libra

A more idealistic, abstract brand of thinking: Analytical, Futuristic, Perfectionistic, Independent.

It is crucial that you understand the following in order to fully comprehend the true nature of the Thinking Signs.

Thinkers are not devoid of emotion by any means! The issue is not that they lack feelings, or that they do not experience all human emotions. It is simply that the Thinking Sign person is not as comfortable in feeling feelings and coping with emotions as is the Feeler.

Because of this, Thinkers have a strong instinctive need to avoid too much emotion. This can make Thinkers seem unemotional. They are not unemotional; they may tend to appear that way due to the discomfort they often feel with showing or expressing emotion. This inability to interact emotionally on a level that is so necessary to the Feelers causes Feelers to perceive Thinkers as being unemotional. It's as if a Thinker does not always have access to his or her emotions, is not always able to easily share joy, excitement, sadness, disappointment, or anger. It is, of course, important that negative feelings be voiced as well as positive ones. It is necessary for one's mate to know virtually everything that one is feeling in order to have an emotionally healthy relationship.

The Mental Sign individuals will make every attempt to remove themselves from the emotional arena—to remain on the perimeter of where the "emotional action" is taking place. It's as if a little alarm goes off, warning them that they are about to enter an "emotional zone." They don't really want to get their "emotional feet" wet. For instance, if a Mental Sign man is talking to you about your feelings of anger (and he may indeed be willing to do this if you seem adequately under control at the time), he may seem to be sharing his thoughts with you about your anger, rather than his feelings. If he were to become too emotional himself, it would perhaps cause him to feel angry, which is not something he wants to do. On the other hand, an Emotional Sign man, while perhaps not relishing feeling upset, would not have as much of a problem if his talking to you about your feelings caused him to feel some of that emotion as well.

Earth and Air Sign people seem to give less priority to feelings than do Water and Fire Sign people. Living more in the realm of their minds, they are made somewhat uneasy by feelings, which cannot be categorized, organized, or controlled as readily as thoughts. With the Thinking mode being so instinctive to them, they appear to be "thinking" their feelings rather than truly feeling them. When they are sharing how they feel, there may be such a thinking overtone that, by the time they get through describing their thoughts on how they feel, it comes across as a thought rather than a feeling! In some cases, several major planets in the Earth or Air Signs indicate extreme discomfort with the emotional dimension of life. There can be such an inability to relate to emotions that these men seem allergic to emotion!

The Feeler needs to talk about feelings, whereas the Mental Sign person prefers not to delve too much into feelings. The Thinker knows that it doesn't take long for a conversation about feelings to touch upon heavy or negative subject matter. They fear that the raised voices and harsh attitudes which make them so uncomfortable cannot be far behind.

Incidentally, it is not that Thinkers always behave in an unemotional manner; quite the opposite in many cases. Ironically, because of their discomfort with experiencing unpleasant feelings, when forced to deal with them they can become extremely emotional. They are prone to short-circuit when attempting to process too much emotion. There can be a tremendous over-reaction to being confronted with a situation that causes them to feel emotions they would prefer to ignore or even deny.

The Feeling Signs

The Water Signs: Pisces, Cancer, Scorpio

A more gentle, ultra-sensitive brand of feeling: Kind, Understanding, Sympathetic, Compassionate, Forgiving.

* * * * * * *

The Fire Signs: Aries, Leo, Sagittarius

A more passionate and intense brand of feeling: Idealistic, Futuristic, Dynamic, Impulsive, Perfectionistic.

The Emotional Sign person lives for emotion! "Feeling" Sun Signs are simply more comfortable with emotionality and the expression of their feelings. They give more priority to emotion (theirs and yours) than do the Earth and Air Sign individuals. At home in the world of feelings, their way of experiencing emotions is to truly feel their feelings, thereby making you feel them too. The Feeler lives for, thrives on, and experiences emotion in a way that is totally foreign to the nature of a Thinker. Water and Fire people have a great need for emotional interaction and feedback. They seek a real closeness or bond with others, needing to feel emotionally connected to their loved ones. They have an innate ability to feel for another. There is often a greater compassion for the needs and wants of others than the Thinkers are able to express (even though they may indeed feel it). Men who are Feelers tend to be more thoughtful and sharing, both emotionally and materially.

I am sure that all of you Feelers have experienced Thinking Sign people in your life who ran for cover when you were in the middle of re-living some emotional trauma that was suddenly too much for them to deal with. They don't necessarily run from the room in a complete state of panic, but they will feel uneasy or anxious, perhaps interrupting you in mid-feeling with a change of subject.

If you are a woman whose Sun is in an Emotional Sign (Fire or Water), you will be particularly emotionally unfulfilled in a relationship with a man who is a Thinker. Women are basically more emotional and more comfortable with their feelings than men. Most men are simply less able to express their deepest feelings, less at home with their emotional side. They tend to think that it is too feminine to feel and express much emotion. Because men have greater difficulty acknowledging and handling their feelings, even the Emotional Sign men are going to be considerably less comfortable with emotion than the Emotional Sign women. Certainly, a man whose Sun Sign is Mental is going to be that much more removed from comprehending your need for emotional interaction.

An Emotional Sign woman needs to be aware of how readily a Thinking man can appear to be more emotionally oriented than he actually is. He may indeed be quite comfortable initially with expressing emotions that he has thought about and is prepared to present to you in a controlled manner. He may manifest a very sincere, considerate, and sensitive personality that gives you the impression of being at home with emotions. You may feel that you have found an exception to the War Between the Signs.

Guess again! This is not the case! Their basic natures are extremely different when it comes to their approach to the world of emotions.

Certainly, many Thinkers will have major planets in the Emotional Elements, which will make them seem more emotional at times. And many Feelers will have planets in the Thinking Elements, which will make them very mental in many respects. But a Thinker is a Thinker and a Feeler is a Feeler!

Thinkers and Feelers are definitely cut from different emotional cloth. While the Feeler is at home in his world of feelings, the Thinker is on the outside looking in through the window, frequently dismayed or unnerved by what he observes.

The Thinker is usually ill at ease with too much display of emotion—not just publicly, and not just screaming or arguing. Even demonstrating the level of positive, loving emotions required by the Emotional Sign people can make Thinkers uncomfortable.

For example, if you are upset about a problem, the Thinker's first instinct will be to deal, not with your being upset, but with the problem. We know that men have a basic urge to solve problems. Therefore, a man who is a Thinker—whose first instinct is to deal with facts, figures, and information—makes for a double whammy! This guy is going to cruise right past your feelings and go straight to problem solving. How can we even be mad at him for it? It is so instinctive that it absolutely does not occur to him to do otherwise. And, even after he has jumped in with all of his practical, helpful suggestions as to how you can efficiently handle the dilemma at hand, he will probably not offer any emotionally supportive comments, such as, "I'm so sorry that you're upset," or perhaps, "Here, let me hold you."

It would probably go more like this: "You're upset because you're not thinking rationally about the situation," or, "If you had obtained all the facts before getting involved in this . . ."

I am not suggesting that there is not a Thinking Sign man in the whole world who is comfortable with "emotional talk." There would be two factors at work to produce this: his chart would probably have the moon and/or one or more of the functional planets (Mercury, Venus, and Mars) in the Emotional Elements of Fire or Water, and he would have had the good fortune to have experienced conversations about feelings wherein there were no serious injuries, leading him to conclude that talking about feelings was not so scary after all. However, remember that this man, who may be more adept at talking about emotion (usually only when he's in the mood) than the average Mental Sign man, is still not on your overall emotional wavelength. Everything discussed in this chapter about Thinking men will still apply to him!

Because a woman who is a Feeler needs an emotionally demonstrative lover, it is very difficult for her to feel loved by a Mental Sign man, who is simply unable to readily express his feelings in ways that are important to her. The typical thinker's inability to converse about feelings can be really devastating to an Emotional Sign woman.

When it comes to starting a relationship, you need a man who can jump in emotionally with both feet (especially if you are a Fire Sign). A Thinker who sits around pondering the feasibility of it all is not for you! And when there are problems in the relationship, the Mental Sign man will not want to know about your need to dissect the relationship in terms of emotional needs and motivations. Perhaps the best way to describe the typical Mental Sign man is simply to say that he suffers from emotional timidity, lacking the bold, dynamic, fearless approach that Fire Sign women desperately need, and that many Water Sign women thrive on as well. It all boils down to a certain emotional aloofness—a feeling that he is there for you one minute, and not the next (particularly true of a Thinker with high Air influence). This type of behavior makes Water Sign women particularly insecure.

Eastern Hemisphere Influence of Mental Sign Men

If his Sign is one of the Mental Signs in the Eastern Hemisphere (Capricorn, Aquarius, Taurus, Gemini), he will tend to function more in terms of self, while the Mental Signs in the Western Hemisphere Signs (Virgo and Libra) are more immediately aware of the needs of others.

The Thinking man is, by nature, less responsive to the emotional needs of others. When these two factors are combined in a chart (particularly if all of his major planets are in the Eastern Hemisphere), it can produce a man who is very self-indulgent and emotionally removed. Certainly, this type of chart will impact negatively on an Emotional Sign woman who needs to feel that a man is sincerely at the other end of the relationship and genuinely concerned with her needs. You will knock yourself out for this guy, and not only will he not appreciate it, but he will feel pressured, thinking that he might have to reciprocate at some future time (and worse yet, maybe at a time when he's not in the mood or has other plans).

When a Thinker perceives himself as being pressured to relate in ways that he cannot, it is not uncommon for him to label you as an overly emotional woman who is insecure and, therefore, too demanding of his attention and affection.

The following conversations illustrate the two worst Element clashes of the zodiac:

PISCES: "You don't understand me and you never will. You think you know me, but you don't know how I feel. You accuse me of being overly emotional, of not being able to control my feelings. At least I *have* feelings! All you ever do is *think* about feelings. Do you always have to analyze everything to death?"

AQUARIUS: "There you go again, having one of your emotional outbursts over nothing. I was just trying to suggest a more rational approach to analyzing the situation at hand, thereby helping you to organize your thoughts and put them into perspective."

ARIES: "Do you always have to be so logical and practical about everything? Are you a person or a computer? This is a relationship, not a business transaction! Even when you say you understand my feelings, you give me your top ten reasons why I shouldn't feel that way! Do you ever just feel something without it having to make sense?"

TAURUS: "If you weren't so intensely emotional and didn't think you were so right all the time, you might be able to calm down and view things a little less emotionally for a change. When I offer you sound advice, I am only attempting to give you a logical overview of the situation. If you don't wish to be practical about life, of course that is your prerogative."

If either of these interchanges sound familiar, perhaps you have been interacting with men whose response to feeling is vastly different than your own. I simply cannot state it strongly enough: these men are not on your emotional planet! It's as though your radio receives one station very clearly (he gets static on that station) and you hear nothing but static on his station.

One of the reasons that it is so difficult for Thinking men to be emotionally supportive, to comfort you when you are upset, is that they cannot relate to why you are allowing yourself to feel emotion to this degree. They do not understand how you can let yourself indulge in feeling your emotions in a way that they would never do. They may even view Feelers as weak or undisciplined. They tend to assume that all mature people should at least strive toward their controlled approach to dealing with emotion.

In other types of relationships, in which emotional closeness is not as crucial, this lack of emotional rapport would not be so critical an issue. Romantic involvements, however, which are based on a couple's ability to bond emotionally, require the same fundamental approach to processing and handling emotions. Without this similarity, it is impossible to build true emotional intimacy.

Notes to the Mental Sign Woman

If you are a Thinking Sign woman (Earth or Air), I can almost hear you thinking, "It might work out quite well for a man to be a Feeling Sign, since men are less emotional anyway; wouldn't this help him to be more emotional?" A good question, but it doesn't work out that way. Emotional opposites may "attract," but they are not compatible! A Feeling Sign man will not be happy unless he is with someone who will help him to express his feelings. The fact that men are busily suppressing their feelings makes it even more important that these men interact with Fire or Water Sign women. This type of woman will understand them emotionally and help them feel more at ease with sharing their feelings in a way that is natural to them. A Thinking Sign woman (all this emotional stuff not being her thing) will make matters even worse for this poor man. He will now be getting an expanded version of the message he has been receiving from the world all his life: "It is wrong for men to show too much emotion." Now he is hearing that it is apparently wrong for *anyone* to show too much emotion!

Again, I can hear a Thinking woman wondering, "Will it make much difference to me if a man is not perfectly happy with my responding to his *every* emotional need?" The answer is that it will make a very great deal of difference to you if the man in your life is not emotionally fulfilled and happy. If both parties are not content within a relationship, then neither party is happy. You will undoubtedly end up feeling pressured by his emotional needs, perhaps labeling him as a baby who needs too much attention. It is not just a matter of your not responding to his every need for a tender expression of your love. We are talking about two totally different approaches to sharing and expressing emotion.

He will tend to label you as emotionally distant and removed and uncaring about his feelings. Is that what you want? Of course not! You want a man who will actually appreciate the very quality in you that might make a Fire Sign man label you as cold. You need a man who loves the fact that you are not always wanting to have emotionally charged conversations about your relationship, sharing and exploring every aspect of your feelings. For instance, I have seen the relief when an Earth Sign man and woman have finally found each other. They were emotionally drained after having both just come out of relationships with highly emotional Fire and Water Sign individuals. These people were eternally grateful to have finally found a fellow Earth Sign soul mate who was not, by their way of thinking, emotionally demanding and always whining about unmet needs and hurt feelings. Different strokes for different folks, kids!

It takes enough precious energy to work at the relationships we have with family members that involve this emotional clash. We can grow and learn from these situations, but we certainly do not need to deal with this in the one relationship where we most yearn to be understood, accepted, and loved by someone on our own emotional wavelength, someone who deals with emotion in the same way we do.

Will Any Two People Whose Sun Signs Do Not Clash Be Emotionally Compatible?

No. Although individuals who both have either Thinking or Feeling Sun Signs share the way in which they deal with the issue of emotionality, this is only a starting point in terms of being able to have a positive relationship. An emotionally healthy, intimate relationship must encompass many other factors as well, ranging from other chart compatibility factors to levels of emotional maturity.

Why Do Some Thinkers Seem So Much Like Feelers Initially, and Vice Versa?

Why is it that some people do not readily appear to be the Mental or Emotional Sign that they are? This is explained by looking at the Elements of the three planets that govern much of our actions. How typical a person is as a Thinker or Feeler will be determined by whether their functional planets back up their Sun Sign. The functional planets are: Mercury, which governs how we think; Venus, which governs how we love; and Mars, which governs how we act. These planets will certainly have an effect on how emotional a man may appear.

Therefore, an Emotional Sun Sign (Fire or Water) man with functional Mental planets may at first appear to be more of a Thinker. A Fire Sign man might be relating to you from his Thinking planets, rather than jumping in the way one might assume that a Fire Sign man would. He may be somewhat hesitant to show or express the Fire or Water nature of his Sign. Yet this individual is still only emotionally compatible with a fellow Emotional Sign.

On the other hand, a Thinking Sign man with functional Emotional planets might initially appear to be more of a Feeler. When an Earth Sign man has Mercury, Venus, and Mars all in the Emotional Element of Fire, he may not seem like a typical Thinker. He will, especially during courtship, be more spontaneous and impulsive in some of his behavior. However, this does not mean that he is not a Thinker when it comes to his innate discomfort with emotionality and the profound ways in which he differs from the Feeler in processing emotions.

How Does the Thinker-Feeler Clash Affect Other Types of Relationships?

The same issues exist with the Thinker-Feeler clash, regardless of the nature of the relationship. Naturally, intimate relationships are impacted more by this clash. (For more information on this clash within families, see Chapter 17: When Parents and Children Have Clashing Signs.)

Picture two girlfriends having lunch. The Emotional Sign woman has a problem that she is upset about. Her Mental Sign friend may try to help by analyzing the situation or offering practical advice. It's obviously fine to do this after genuinely listening and offering emotional support. But the Thinking friend ought to make every attempt to initially ignore the facts of the issue itself, and concentrate on how her friend feels about the situation.

When the Mental Sign friend has a problem, she needs to have support offered, but without too much emotional intensity. She prefers to have a calm, pleasant, productive conversation that doesn't become too emotional.

This clash can also manifest itself in the arena of "girl talk." Emotional Sign women love to talk about how they feel about things. If an interesting new man has come into her life, she can't wait to share all of the exciting details with her best friend. Much of the conversation will revolve around how she feels about him, how he makes her feel, and how happy she feels. If she is a Fire Sign, she may leave no superlative unturned: he is marvelous, wonderful, incredible, unbelievable, fabulous!

How will the Earth or Air Sign woman tell you about her new love? She is generally more reserved or dignified in her attitude toward life, avoiding emotionally charged descriptions of her feelings. She will be even less inclined to wax emotional about private matters such as a new beau. She will be more prone to talk about what a good job he has, how intelligent he is, and how much they have in common. At times, an Earth or Air Sign woman can be very effusive, sharing her feelings in a way that will remind you of an Emotional Sign woman. If she has major Fire planets in her chart, she may indeed use some of the Fire superlatives: he has a wonderful job and is incredibly intelligent, and it's unbelievable how much they have in common!

Can a Couple Have a Healthy Relationship Despite a Thinker-Feeler Clash?

In extremely rare cases, when both individuals are very emotionally mature and very much in love, and when their charts do not show major clashes and reflect very positive factors (how often do we find all of these ingredients?), they can sometimes overcome the basic differences in their emotional natures.

How Thinkers and Feelers Approach New Relationships?

The Feeling Couple

For this example, both parties are Fire Signs with functional Fire planets.

These two will jump in with both feet—no stop signs or road blocks in sight! With Fire Signs being the most comfortable with emotions and their expression, this pair will usually not have a problem in responding to each other's indication of interest. They will soon be giving each other cards, flowers, and other expressions of undying love and devotion. Neither one will probably remember who first blurted out, "I love you, and I cannot imagine life having any meaning without your love!" There is, of course, a big potential problem area here: too much too soon! When a Fire Sign individual enters into situations with such wild abandon, and then has another "relationship junkie" at the other end, moderation is unfortunately not in their vocabulary (see Chapter 7: Is He an Emotional Grownup?).

Is there such a thing as "love at first sight"? Would any couple ever be so astrologically suited to each other that it could make sense to instantly enter into an exclusive relationship? Never! No matter how well matched the two charts may be or how incredible the chemistry and rapport is, there would be a great risk in terms of the ultimate outcome of the relationship. In Chapter 18: Somewhere Out There, I cover in detail the drawbacks of becoming involved too quickly.

The Thinking Couple

For this example, both people are Earth Signs.

If these two are portrayed in a movie, you might want to go out for popcorn during the first half of the film; you won't miss much! While it depends upon all of the exact chart influences, Mental Sign people are not known for eagerly jumping into relationships, especially romantic ones. Emotions can be scary. They have to properly consider, analyze, and review everything adequately before making a decision to act on their feelings. This is all well and good, to a point. Let us look at what can happen if one of these people does not manage to activate the other person's Fire (more about that later) before they fall asleep or think that the other one is not interested in them.

I have seen this happen many times. It goes something like this: boy meets girl; boy asks girl out; girl accepts; they go out. They are very attracted to each other. But being the dignified Earth or Air Signs that they are, neither boy nor girl makes a move or even really flirts with the other. Perhaps, in her case, she thinks that it should be up to the man to make the first move.

Now bear in mind that these two are very attracted to each other. Why does the gentleman in question not make a move? There may be any number of reasons. Maybe he is insecure with women, and helps protect himself from possible rejection by not acting until he gets a definite signal. Perhaps he is being respectful of her, if she has just come out of a relationship, and he thinks that she may not be ready for that type of involvement yet. Whatever the reason, these people can miss each other as surely as if one of them had been given the wrong address for their first meeting. Each person walks away from a situation like this thinking that the other party obviously did not find him or her to be irresistible. This is not necessarily the case. They were both resisting simply because they were being so mental about everything and were too busy thinking of all the reasons why it might not be advisable for them to act on their feelings or urges at this time.

What a waste! Their charts might have been incredibly well matched, and they could have had a fabulous relationship! However, Thinkers often fail to use the Fire in their charts to activate the other person's Fire and get things cooking. This is due to their fundamental discomfort with feelings which are not totally predictable and controllable. And they tend to think too much without acting. All it might have taken was for one of them to be just flirtatious enough to make it clear to the other that he or she was interested!

You might think that things would go better if we took a Fire person, who could get things going, and put him or her with an Earth person, who is so emotionally cautious. Wrong! Unfortunately, this is precisely what often happens; hence, back to the "opposites attract" theory. It is not so much that they "attract," it's just that it may be the Emotional people who get things happening due to their natural urge to act on what they feel. But what good does it do them to activate a Mental Sign person, whose entire attitude, approach, and ability to handle and express emotion is totally different from their own? The Thinking people may initially respond favorably, due to the fact that they are involved in courtship behavior with lots of happy feelings that they feel somewhat safe in expressing. However, when the euphoria dies down and the Feeler finds that he or she needs more emotional feedback on a daily basis than the Thinker is comfortable providing, that is when the problems start. A Thinker and a Feeler can rarely work through the tough times in a productive way. Even when they do, there will always be that lingering feeling that the other party does not truly understand them. Emotionally clashing Signs are simply at opposite ends of the emotional scale.

A Final Look at Our Thinking Couple
Let's say that this couple has finally managed to activate their Fire, and are experiencing their first weekend together. Actually, there is a true story of just such a couple that is unfolding just as I am editing this chapter. Today is Valentine's Day; is the

Earth couple celebrating this day of such romantic significance by strolling on the beach after having had a lovely champagne brunch? No, Carol and Darryl are busily making a list for their trip to Home Depot. They are then planning on an afternoon of barn repairs. Ah, romance, ain't it grand? But finally the Fire comes into play: he gave her a beautiful gold heart pendant, and they have planned a romantic dinner for tonight!

A Final Note

While potential emotional compatibility exists between two Mental Sign people or two Emotional Sign people, the potential for compatibility and emotional rapport is even greater between individuals of the same Element. Two Fire people will share a brand of Fire passion unknown to the other Elements; two Water Signs, a type of gentle sensitivity unique to their Element. Earth individuals share a grounded Earthy logic, while the Air couple has an original, futuristic brand of thinking.

In order to fully understand the emotional nature of the four Elements and to learn about the crucially important part they play in our relationships, see Chapter 4: The Matches and the Mismatches. This chapter truly captures the essence of the emotional rapport, or lack thereof, between any two Elements.

4

The Matches and the Mismatches

The Matches

The couples I will describe in this section are similar to each other in their approach to emotions, and in their comfort zones in terms of handling and processing their feelings.

Couples Whose Sun Signs Are in the Feeling Elements

People with Sun Signs in Water and Fire are fundamentally comfortable with emotion and tend to base decisions on how they feel.

A Fire Sign with a Fire Sign

This couple shares the passion and intensity of the most confident and dynamic of the elements, the one most comfortable with expressing emotion: Fire! Their romantic approach to life will be idealistic and futuristic. They will always be looking for ways to enhance their relationship, and each one will tend to confront the other with his or her feelings. While the other Elements are sometimes overwhelmed by Fire's intensity, these two will relate well to one another's fiery and passionate nature.

A Water Sign with a Water Sign

These individuals will relate to each other with a greater display of gentle sensitivity and consideration for the other party than any other combination of Elements. They are both highly tuned in to each other's feelings and sincerely interested in meeting their mutual emotional needs. A Water Sign person really needs a fellow Water Sign. It is very difficult for someone of another Element to fully understand Water's brand of sensitive emotionality. There will be a sincere demonstration of affection between these two.

A Fire Sign with a Water Sign

With this couple, we have a combination of the two Feeling Elements. The Fire individual will be more dynamically romantic and show more intense emotion; the Water individual will approach the relationship with more subtle feelings and ultra-sensitivity.

While both parties are fundamentally comfortable with emotion, the Fire Sign person is much more so, and will be more confrontive with his or her feelings. The emotional compatibility between these Elements will be enhanced if each person has planets in the other's Element: Water would have some of Fire's brand of emotion, and Fire would possess Water's sensitivity.

Couples Whose Sun Signs Are
in the Thinking Elements

Earth and Air Signs are somewhat uncomfortable with too much emotional display, and need to be more in control of their feelings.

An Air Sign with an Air Sign

Air Sign individuals have very romantic souls, and will approach relationships and life in general with dignity and ultra-sensitivity. They are direct, inquisitive, communicative, and restless, with a real need for variety. Because, in this case, both partners have a need to be in control of their emotions, they will solve any differences by analyzing things in a rational and civilized manner. And each party will understand the other's need to be alone; though they love to interact with others, there is a great need for "alone time." Unlike people of other elements, these two will not view each other's need for emotional independence as cold or distant.

An Earth Sign with an Earth Sign
These individuals will share a practical attitude toward life and love, and both will approach a relationship with a good deal of caution and reserve. While Earth Sign people may indeed possess romantic qualities through their other planet placements, their basic way of operating within a love relationship is more earthy. The realistic Earth Sign woman will appreciate the Earth Sign gentleman's gesture or gift, which may lack the ultimate romantic flair but will always be thoughtful and useful. These two will not be saying to each other, "What about feelings? You're always being logical and practical!"

An Air Sign with an Earth Sign
While Air is more impulsive than Earth, both will need to feel emotionally "safe" before entering into a relationship. These Thinking Signs share a dislike of highly emotional exchanges, preferring to discuss things in a rational (Air) and logical (Earth) manner. Ideally, this match would find each party having planets in the other's Element, in order that the Air individual could relate to Earth's more practical nature, and the Earth individual might better understand Air's abstract, analytical style of thinking.

The Mismatches

With each of the following couples, there is a clash between the thinking and the Feeling Elements. People with their Sun Signs in the Feeling Elements of Fire and Water are more comfortable with emotion, and those in the Thinking Elements of Earth and Air are less comfortable with emotion.

An Air Sign with a Fire Sign
Fate plays tricks with us here. Air and Fire are often attracted to one another, but this is a definite clash. While both Elements are romantic, creative, idealistic, and futuristic, Fire's passion and intensity will ultimately result in the more reserved Air person feeling anxious, overwhelmed, and restricted. The emotional independence of Air does not mesh well with Fire's need to almost possess his or her mate emotionally. The Fire person will feel unfulfilled by what he or she perceives as a lack of enough dynamic show of passion and undying devotion, and will probably accuse the Air person of being cold and removed.

An Air Sign with a Water Sign
Air and Water people are both ultrasensitive, and will be attracted to that quality in each another. But their similarity ends there. In spite of their great sensitivity, Air Sign individuals will be perceived as having a removed or controlling attitude by the highly emotional Water Signs. The Air party will invariably perceive the Water person's emotional neediness as interfering with his or her need for space and independence. The Water person's need to "become one emotionally" with a mate is something that the extremely emotionally independent Air Sign simply cannot understand.

An Earth Sign with a Fire Sign
The clash between these two Elements is one of the worst. The emotional intensity and impulsiveness of Fire is very different from the more reserved emotional nature of Earth. Fire is the Element most comfortable with emotion and confrontation, while Earth is the least comfortable with emotion and confrontation. Earth Sign people (especially Virgos) will invariably feel criticized by Fire Sign people (especially Aries). Earth Sign people can become very annoyed by Fire's extravagant nature

and impulsiveness, and Fire is often bored by what is perceived as a lack of romance and spontaneity in the Earth person.

An Earth Sign with a Water Sign

It is very difficult for the more emotionally cautious and less romantic Earth Sign individual to understand the ultrasensitive emotional nature of the Water Sign person. The Earth individual's more earthy and matter-of-fact approach tends to run roughshod over the Water person's need for a more gentle and tender expression of love. The Earth person will often perceive the Water individual's normal level of emotional neediness as weakness, immaturity, and a lack of emotional strength.

5

Why Can't a Man Be
More Like a Woman?

Why is it that some men actually understand that we may just want to talk about something without instantly looking for a solution? Why are some men so much more sensitive, loving, and attuned to our needs? Because these men have more feminine energy in their charts.

The ancient Orientals referred to the masculine and feminine energies as yin and yang. The men who possess more gentle and caring qualities have more of the feminine, or Yin, energies in their charts. The men who think they rule the world have an overdose of masculine, or Yang, energy. Fortunately, the science of astrology allows us to immediately determine the balance of masculine and feminine energy in a person's chart. This affords you the opportunity to resist a man who might have seemed irresistible before you had this knowledge. Now you know that what seemed like a refreshing take-charge demeanor was actually the manifestation of an overly masculine chart.

After many centuries during which the sexes were virtually clueless as to each other's needs, we have the good fortune to be living at a time when we are beginning to understand the tremendous differences between the genders. Dr. John Gray, in *Men Are From Mars, Women Are From Venus*, captures the essence of the differences between men and women, and between male and female energies, which Dr. Gray refers to as

"Martian" and "Venusian." He explains what astrology shows us: that we all have masculine and feminine energies within us. He also talks about the importance of learning to blend these energies, striving to be more of a "Marusian."

When a chart is well balanced—meaning that it has similar numbers of planets in the feminine (Water and Earth) Elements and the masculine (Fire and Air) Elements—a person has the good fortune of being a natural-born Marusian, with a balance of the Martian and Venusian Elements. However, even these individuals can have difficulty manifesting these behaviors in a well-integrated manner. Envision these energies floating around in a big pot. They need to be stirred constantly so that they do not separate. Within a particular conversation, one may show a more calm and gentle side (Venusian), and then make a point with a more dynamic and assertive attitude (Martian).

Unfortunately, this is a problem for most of us. We are either using too much masculine (Martian) energy and are too aggressive and intense, or too much feminine (Venusian) energy and are too passive and nonconfrontive. A high percentage of the population either shrugs things off, avoiding confrontation when it seems uncomfortable, or comes on too strong, aggressive, and angry. In a given situation, we may either care too much about the other person's needs (Venusian), or disregard their needs and think only about our own desires (Martian). Why is it so difficult to blend these parts of ourselves? It is as though we become instantly hypnotized by either our masculine or feminine side, and proceed as though the other part of us does not exist.

Perhaps the single greatest indicator of whether a person is adult, functioning, and emotionally mature is his or her ability to effectively blend Yin and Yang, and thereby manifest the gender energy appropriate for the occasion.

I would now like to describe Martian and Venusian energy in a way that I hope will capture the essence of the innate attitude and behavior patterns that are so instinctive and unique to that gender. I have chosen to refer to this gender issue with the terms "Martian" and "Venusian" because the terms "masculine" and "feminine" are too well-defined in our language to be easily understood in this new context. For example, when I refer to a man's chart as having a strong "Venusian" influence, rather than saying "feminine" influence, there is less likelihood of confusion regarding his sexual preference.

Rarely will a given man manifest innate Martian traits in pure form. This is because most men have some Venusian energies as a result of having planets in the feminine Elements of Earth and Water (though, Lord knows, we occasionally run across a gentleman who does a convincing impersonation of someone with 100-percent Martian energy).

Of course, there are some men and women who typify the classic behavior of their gender: the Super-Martian, the man (referred to above) with extremely high Air/Fire influence, and the Super-Venusian woman with all major planets in the Earth or Water Signs.

We will look more fully at how this highly imbalanced gender energy plays havoc with an individual after we look at gender energies in their pure, raw form.

In the following explanation of masculine and feminine energies, I will avoid the constant repetition of the word "energy" after the terms "Martian" and "Venusian," and I will use these terms in singular form. For example, "Martian likes to be in control," rather than, "Martians like to be in control," may help reinforce the fact that I am talking about the Elements of Air and Fire (Martian Elements) that like to be in control. I am seeking to avoid the implication that all men like to be in control, because all of us are a blend of the Martian and Venusian attitudes and behaviors. Many women reading the description of Martian energy will recognize their pronounced Martian side, particularly those with their Sun, moon, and two or more additional major planets in Air or Fire Signs. Both men and women with heavy Martian influences need to work at developing their Venusian side in order to become more balanced in their approach to life—in order to become Marusian. Each individual needs a healthy manifestation of both genders to function successfully in the world.

Martian Energy:
Self-Oriented, Masculine, Confrontive

The Martian view of the world is focused, as opposed to the expansive view of the Venusian. Martian energy zeroes in on one issue, fact, or project, and does not instinctively look at the whole picture. Venusian energy is the opposite, seeing many aspects of the situation at once.

The two greatest Martian needs are to be appreciated and to be admired.

The planet Mars rules the masculine Sign of Aries (Fire) and is the planet of war and of action. Martian needs to take charge and make things happen! Martian is goal-oriented and thrives on problem solving. This masculine energy needs to produce results! This is why Martian jumps in so eagerly when someone is talking about a problem. Martian is looking to immediately solve the problem. I say "immediately" because Martian is also impatient. The other person may need to just talk about his or her feelings; Martian needs to jump in, find a sense of direction, and arrive at a plan of action. Martian's innate urge to focus can result in an inability to see other contributing factors.

Frustration is another Martian trait. Martian gets frustrated when someone becomes upset with the proposed quick-fix program. Martian is result-oriented, and self-esteem is greatly affected by the ability or inability to produce results. Is it any wonder that Martian needs to take control? And since the most important result that Martian wants to achieve is another's happiness, it is a double whammy if you are upset and Martian is unable to do anything about it. Actually, this is a triple whammy: Martian needs to produce results, make you happy, and be admired and appreciated. Without this, Martian virtually dies emotionally. And yet the person Martian needs to help is even more upset, due to the Martian way of handling things.

Martian is now totally devastated! If not appreciated and admired, Martian assumes that it is because satisfactory results have not been produced.

In fact, when a lover, friend, or family member has had their feelings hurt, the Martian individual tends to focus on the fact that he or she is not being adequately appreciated at that moment. This suddenly becomes the emphasis, and another Martian trait comes into play: the urge to defend! Martian hates to be wrong, so surely it must be the other person who is wrong. Therefore, Martian now gives all the reasons why the other person must be mistaken, perhaps followed by comments about their oversensitivity.

The Martian within us dislikes unsolicited advice and direction (a woman with a very strong Air/Fire influence may find this to be as distasteful as a man does). Believe it or not, when Martian feels unable to get you from Point A to Point B singlehandedly, the subconscious thought is, "How can we ever get to where we need to go in life if I can't get us to the mall?"

Anger is Martian. When one is assertive, aggressive, or filled with righteous indignation, it is emanating from Martian energy. Impatience, intolerance, and a tendency to be judgmental are Martian traits. One can see how some of these Martian instincts might add up to a spoiled-child mentality.

The Martian Elements of Air and Fire produce a powerful brand of creativity that focuses on changing the world; it is ingenious, inventive, and original. When the brilliance and imagination of Air ignites the intense confidence and electric emotion of Fire, it gives us a dynamic form of creativity that looks idealistically to the future for the good of all humanity.

Venusian Energy:
Other-Oriented, Feminine, Nonconfrontive

The Venusian view of the world is expansive, instinctively seeing both the positive and negative sides of everything, as opposed to the focused view of the Martian. Venusian is expanded consciousness, seeing the entire scope of the situation and all of the related parts. Martian is the opposite, focusing in on one aspect of the situation.

The two greatest Venusian needs are to be heard and to be understood!

Remember that the following description of Venusian energy refers to the feelings, thoughts, urges, desires, and instinctive traits that are produced in any individual (male or female) as a result of the planets in his or her chart that are found in the feminine Elements of the Water and Earth Signs.

Venus, the feminine planet of love and beauty, rules the Sign of Taurus. Venusian is loving, caring, understanding, and sympathetic. This gentle, kind energy is supportive and nurturing. There is a profound need to help and rescue those in need. The part of us that wants to help a homeless person is Venusian. Yet it is crucial to have both feminine and masculine energy within us, because it is the Martian part of us that will put a plan into action—to go forth and build a shelter for the homeless. And, while Martian wants it done yesterday, it is Venusian's patience and perseverance that helps see the project through.

Martian/Venusian Balance

Are you starting to see how well the masculine and feminine energies work together, how much they need each other? The Venusian part of us sees the whole picture, then our Martian side narrows it down and deals with the particular issue of importance at that moment.

Martian's penchant for both efficiency and laziness produces a desire to do no more than required. This may seem confusing, based on the fact that Martian is so action-oriented, with such a need to produce results, but it actually makes a great deal of sense. The need is to put the effort where it will produce the greatest result, and to conserve energy for where it is perceived to be needed. Martian is like someone with a great deal of money to spend but who is very selective about where to spend it.

Venusian is the exact opposite of lazy. There seems to be an endless desire to do everything for everybody. Venusian thrives on love, beauty, and kindness. There is an overpowering urge for everything to be pleasant and agreeable. Venusian cannot stand to hurt anyone's feelings. Venusian would often prefer to just let it go rather than saying something that might hurt another person. Therefore, the Venusian way of confronting can be subtly criticizing. Sometimes the criticism is not so subtle though; the unevolved Venusian energy can be very whining and complaining.

While Martian (Air/Fire) is the honest, candid part of us, the Venusian (Earth/Water) part of us may not want to face the truth. The truth can be ugly. Venusian hates ugly; Venusian is a lover of beauty. Martian is confrontive energy; Venusian is nonconfrontive energy. When someone with predominantly Venusian planets confronts someone else, he or she will be doing so as Martian—perhaps from their only planet in Air or Fire. Whether a person is basically more confrontive or more nonconfrontive will depend upon the exact number of planets in the Martian and Venusian Elements.

Martian/Venusian Imbalances

What Happens When a Man's Chart Is Too Venusian?

Men with an extremely high influence in the feminine Elements of Earth and Water will be very different from the average man. This strong Venusian influence can present almost as many problems for a man as it does for a woman with too much feminine influence in her chart (see Are You Too Venusian? below). Strong Venusians can be imbalanced in terms of their concern for others, their need to please others, and their worrying about what others think of them. These individuals can be so overly loving, caring, sympathetic, helpful, agreeable, and nurturing that they are imbalanced without even knowing it. These energies are so instinctive to them that they may not have a clue that they are functioning in this way or that there is any problem in doing so.

A highly Venusian man may have difficulty facing things straight on and being completely truthful. The Venusian energies can make this man so nonconfrontive that he is apt to do or say anything to avoid conflict, to make things go smoothly. There is a powerful Venusian urge to not make waves or hurt anyone!

These men with too many planets in the Earth and Water Signs really need to learn to operate from whatever Martian energy (Fire or Air) they have in their charts in order to balance themselves in terms of this gender issue.

Unfortunately, it can be difficult to manifest these Martian energies with grace. When a man has such a strong Venusian influence in his chart, he may sense that he needs to be "more of a man." This can cause him to be overly masculine when he acts from his Fire or Air planets. His behavior may be erratic and unpredictable. While his basic manner and personality may be too agreeable, too nurturing, too inclined to worry about everyone else, he can, in an instant, become controlling and demanding, insistent that things be done his way. It is as though he feels that when he is operating from the Martian energy, he needs to somehow make up for the fact that he is usually too accommodating to everyone else's needs. It can take a great deal of work and effort to even out this imbalance. Also, the man who is too Venusian can be particularly irritating, complaining, and spoiled if he was spoiled as a child.

While women can be drawn to such men with their gentle brand of sensitivity—to men who are on their basic Venusian wavelength—and while they may appreciate the kind, gentle, nice-guy part of him, they tend to feel more passion for the man with more dynamic Martian energy.

Are You Too Venusian?

If a woman's chart has most of its major planets in Earth and Water, she may be too passive, compromising, forgiving, and accommodating.

Even a woman with a good overall balance of Elements can be too Venusian. Since she is Venusian by virtue of being female, all she needs is to have her Sun Sign and perhaps only one other major planet in Water or Earth to make her too subservient to men, too agreeable, and too willing to set her own needs aside for others.

This is extremely unhealthy in any relationship, for two basic reasons. First, any mature, evolved man wants a woman who will stand up for herself—a woman who respects herself. Second, a woman who does too much for a man throws the male-female relationship out of balance; a man feels like a child who is unable to do things for himself when a woman is constantly nurturing, waiting on, and fussing over him.

Men sincerely want to do things for women, but we must learn to ask for what we want. The Water or Earth Sign woman often has a particularly hard time asking for what she needs. The overly Venusian women (or even men) with this imbalance tend to feel that they do not even deserve the thing in the first place. No wonder they have a hard time asking for it! There is often almost an "excuse me for living" attitude—a feeling of "who am I to expect . . . ?"

Venusians seem to have an overpowering urge to put everyone's needs above their own. Big mistake! There is nothing more detrimental to your own health and well-being. Women with an extreme chart influence in the Venusian Elements virtually live for others: what they think, what they want, what they need. It can be unbelievably difficult to fight the urge to always help others, to care so much about what others think; "others" is the name of the game! But the entire game plan needs to change drastically: *you* have to become the game. You have to reinvent yourself and learn to live for *you!* We all need to develop our Martian Elements of Air and Fire, which enable us to be confrontive, assertive, or even demanding when necessary. The Air and Fire energies within us give us the feeling that we have the right to want and to insist upon what we need.

When Either Sex Is Too Venusian

The greatest problem faced by those who are too Venusian is nonconfrontiveness. Often the most important person not being confronted is oneself. If we cannot confront ourselves about what we need and what we want, the odds are that no one else will be doing it for us. Ultimately, the inability to confront oneself results in one of the real inhibitors to personal growth: denial.

If one is careful not to bring to the conscious mind anything that one would rather not address, there is no risk of being upset with oneself for not having the willpower to work on it. Unfortunately, those who indulge in denial on a regular basis suffer emotionally and physically from the stress that results from suppressing issues and feelings that desperately need to be dealt with.

Just as nonconfrontiveness can lead to denial, a natural result of denial can be lying, whether to oneself or to another. One cannot very well tell the truth if one does not acknowledge or recognize it. Those with this chart imbalance simply do not want to tell you anything that will upset you, thereby perhaps instigating an argument. They will generally wish to avoid this at all cost. When the Water influence is stronger than the Earth in an overly Venusian chart, the distortion of truth may be even more pronounced; Water's imaginative talents may come into play.

While the curiosity and honesty of the masculine Elements of Fire and Air manifest as an urge to seek truth, the energy of the feminine Elements of Water and Earth tends to manifest in the opposite direction. It is not really that the Venusian energies are dishonest, but they lack the powerfully truthful urge of Air and Fire.

A healthy level of disclosure in a relationship is difficult enough for those with a good balance of Air and Fire in their charts. It takes confidence and a strong sense of self for an individual to feel comfortable sharing thoughts and feelings without fear of rejection. It is ever so much more difficult for individuals without enough major planets in the Elements of Air and Fire, which give us the urge to be honest and direct.

When Men Are Too Martian

The Super-Martian—a man whose chart has a very strong Martian influence—can be extremely dysfunctional. When all or most of his major planets are in the masculine Elements, it causes a man to be overly masculine in his attitude and behavior. This abundance of Air or Fire influence produces a highly self-centered, spoiled mentality and an imbalance that we have come to know as "male chauvinism." Unlike Venusian, which innately respects and values others, Martian has an instinctively superior demeanor—a "look at me, I'm the best" attitude. An extremely high Martian influence is a problem due to its total lack of the understanding and forgiving Venusian Elements. (For more information, see Chapter 6: The Male Chauvinist, Astrologically Defined.)

The Super-Martian man will have no major Venusian energies from which he can function; only the dogmatic, self-oriented Martian behavior is instinctive. This man is domineering and perfectionistic, and has little in the way of patience or tolerance (which are Venusian traits). He will have serious problems in the maturity department and, in the worst-case scenario, is sociopathic in his extreme inability to comprehend that other people's needs have any consequence.

Whether or not he has an outwardly arrogant or aggressive personality, the Super-Martian has an enormous ego and desperately needs to achieve and succeed. If life circumstances have caused him to feel inadequate, insecure, or lacking in self-confidence, he will have enormous difficulty coming to terms with the incongruity of the situation. One manifestation of his exaggerated need to feel important will be his attempts to make you feel otherwise.

Too many planets in the Eastern Hemisphere can also contribute to the malfunctioning of strong Martian energy. This adds even more emotional independence and the tendency to focus on one's self rather than on another.

When Women Are Too Martian

If a woman has most of her major planets (Sun, Ascendant, Moon, Mercury, Venus, Mars) in the Martian Elements (Fire and Air Signs), she is likely to have problems similar to those of a man with this chart emphasis. The Venusian influence of gender will help to offset the impact of a strong Martian chart. Certainly the effect will not be as apparent and the demonstration of these traits will not be as strong. However, she will be a very strong-minded individual with a powerful need to be appreciated and admired.

The Martian woman will have an abundance of the positive Martian qualities as well; highly original and creative, she will always have a new and better approach and a desire to change the world. She wants to take charge and make things happen and is confrontive about her needs and feelings.

It can be difficult for a highly Martian woman to find the right man. She needs a man who is very strong and confident. Most women want this, but this woman really needs it. Regrettably, when a man has enough Martian in his chart to meet her needs, he will often be too overly masculine to be tolerable, or he may not be appreciative regarding her creative (Fire/Air) ideas about how to improve the relationship.

Men and Women Respond Differently to Emotional Upsets

Venusian Response

Venusian energy is very different from Martian's more spoiled, impatient attitude and short fuse. The Martian tends to be less tolerant of emotional or physical discomfort, and is quick to respond emotionally.

As surely as Martian retreats to a "cave" when upset, Venusian's mood will swing from positive to negative. The Venusian nonconfrontive nature often results in a woman feeling unsupported and having many unmet needs (she is always doing things for everybody else, but what about her?). There is a great need for the woman with too much Venusian influence to adopt more of Martian's me-first mentality. When a woman has really integrated her Venusian and Martian energies, she is much less prone to this emotional fluctuation, which Dr. John Gray refers to as "self-esteem rising and falling in a wave motion." An ever-present Martian sense of self-worth would enable her to address and meet her needs in a way that a person who is too Venusian simply does not do.

Even when Venusian is in a negative emotional space, there is still an awareness of the other person's feelings. There will always be what I have come to call "arrows of concern" directed at one's mate. This is due to the simple fact that Venusian's first instinct is to care about others. Venusian energy is warm and forgiving, whereas Martian is more distant and judgmental.

Martian Response

The Martian reaction to feeling emotionally upset is very different from the Venusian response. The more easygoing Venusian energy will feel wounded by criticism, while the more intense and perfectionistic Martian energy feels unappreciated and insulted, with a "how dare you" attitude. While Martian has the need to regularly retreat to a cave, when criticized he moves all the way in! He is suddenly not the least bit interested in your needs or feelings.

The Venusian side of this man—which may have shown all the genuine concern in the world for you only moments ago— simply does not exist for the moment (or for hours, days, or weeks)! He has no Venusian arrows of concern for you; his arrows are all aimed in *his* direction! He has tuned you out, and his Martian penchant for focusing on a project is now focused on how *he* feels, on how angry *he* is! You needn't waste your time imagining what feelings of remorse he might be having about hurting you; I assure you, he is not thinking about *you.* If he thinks of you at all, it will be in terms of how you upset him! And Martian energy can be into revenge, so he just may like the idea that you are suffering—after all, you made *him* suffer!

6

The Male Chauvinist, Astrologically Defined

What makes one man Mr. Chauvinist and another man Mr. Sensitive?

Why can't a man be more like a woman when it comes to being considerate and caring? Some men are! (See Chapter 5.) They are gentle, kind, sympathetic, loving, flexible, compassionate, patient, and considerate, if their charts reflect the feminine influence of the Water and Earth Signs. Then there are the other kind: more self-centered, demanding, aggressive, impatient, and controlling. This results from the masculine influence of the Air and Fire Signs. Too many planets in the Martian Signs produces a man who simply has too much masculine energy: the male chauvinist!

Before exploring the chauvinist mentality, let's look at the positive side of Air and Fire. A combination of Air and Fire, particularly in the Sun and Moon Signs, produces individuals without equal in their capacity to communicate emotionally and verbally and in their ability to motivate and inspire others. Air brings its flash insight, intuition, and sensitivity to Fire's dynamic nature and intense passion. Seekers of the truth, in search of self-actualization, Air/Fire people are consumed with growth and the future, with all of its limitless possibilities. Our most talented inventors, writers, public speakers, therapists, and members of the film and music industry will have strong Air and Fire influence in their charts. Air/Fire people are more in need of relationships than the other Element types. They have a great capacity to show both a dynamic and sensitive expression of their love, as well as having a real need for this themselves. Men with solid Fire and Air emphasis (without involving too many planets) can make exciting and wonderful mates!

Incidentally, any man with even one or two major planets in the masculine Elements is capable of being very Martian from time to time. Be patient and try to remember how natural it is for him to jump right in with ideas, to solve every problem, and to instinctively suggest a better way of doing something. Think of it as being protective; what else can the poor dear do, being a Martian by birth and then having all that creative, fix-it Air/Fire energy? Think of it as sort of a "boys will be boys" thing. Picture him "playing Martian," the way he might have played "cowboys and Indians" when he was a kid.

The Super-Martian

And now let us explore the man who has far too many planets in the masculine Signs. Fasten your seat belt for a journey into the mind of the "Super-Martian"—the man from another planet! The man from Mars, who, try as he might, just cannot totally get the concept that women are truly equal to men! This type of man cannot identify with a philosophy that is intrinsically foreign to his deepest subconscious feelings. His thoughts and feelings are possessed by the masculine nature of Fire and Air. His overabundance of masculine energies produces a feeling of male superiority and a macho mentality. Not only does he believe that men are superior, but he perceives women as basically weak and in need of his protection, guidance, and assistance. If his chart is extremely high in the masculine Elements of Fire and Air, his emphasis in the feminine Elements of Water and Earth will be very low, and he will therefore be lacking the feminine Venusian energies (deep sensitive emotion, gentleness, consideration, and empathy).

These men suffer from what I have come to refer to as "overly masculine" behavior. We have all known the type of man who is demanding, aggressive, domineering, opinionated, impatient, and judgmental. He has a need to take charge, to be in control. He will be fiercely independent and very self-centered, and will see everything from his point of view. Depending upon how high the Fire influence is, a man with this problem can be truly overbearing and arrogant—even tyrannical! This masculine influence also produces rash behavior, impulsiveness, and an urge to act at all cost. Men with very high Fire or Air emphasis tend to feel indestructible.

While "Mr. Egomaniac" may stand out from across the room at a social gathering, he often appears incognito, well disguised as an emotionally mature man with whom one could actually have adult interaction and a normal relationship. Sorry! There is nothing "normal" about this fellow. Ironically, some of the symptoms of this ego disease may initially be perceived as positive traits: a man with supreme self-confidence, a "dynamic" man who takes charge, a man who knows what he wants! Unfortunately, one of the things he wants to take charge of is your life, at least insofar as it affects his life. This may initially involve only subtle suggestions, such as a friendly reminder that feeding your cats "people tuna" is a foolish extravagance. How could he have failed to notice that it happened to be 3:00 A.M. and you were out of feline food?

All of the wonderfully thoughtful and considerate courtship behavior that he has been displaying for perhaps a week or two might just be coming to an abrupt halt. Most of these men are not able to suppress their Super-Martian behavior for very long if at all. And the man who is able to initially conceal his emotional infancy will invariably let the cat out of the bag before long. Do you see how crucial it is to know a man before you allow yourself to become emotionally involved? Before long, his irresistible urge to reform you might escalate into some very specific ideas as to how your quality of life would be vastly improved, such as by no longer associating with certain friends of yours whom he has deemed unfit. Oddly enough, this will often include those very friends who have perceived him to be not quite the catch he thinks he is!

Unfortunately, very few women give proper credence to this "handwriting on the wall." When a man whose chart has a high Air/Fire influence begins to show the attitude and traits discussed in this chapter, get out while you are still able to make a decision of this magnitude without his stamp of approval. You should end a relationship with any man who is demonstrating serious overly masculine traits before he shows any sign of the most serious problem these men can have: violent behavior!

A man like this is prone to violence as a result of the level of anger that an Air/Fire individual experiences in comparison to other Element combinations. This stems from the extreme degree of idealism and perfectionism that high Air/Fire men possess. We live in a very unidealistic and imperfect world. Combine these ingredients with Air/Fire's impatience, aggression, a judgmental nature, and need for control, and you have a recipe for uncontrollable rage.

There is an important area to look at with these men. With their ego problems, they have a great need to be financially successful. When a man with this exaggerated male ego feels like a failure, due to lack of education or lack of success in his career, he will be impossible to live with. He will have a rigid attitude when it comes to conversations about money and what he cannot afford to do for you. His feelings of inadequacy about not being able to protect and provide for a woman as he would like to may cause him to short circuit. Air/Fire people are not known for their patience and self-control. Obviously, these very highly masculine-influenced men, who need to be able to provide a woman with protection and security, are particularly upset when they are not able to do so (or at least not according to their standards). With a spoiled-child mentality and a temper problem, this type of man could be described as a time bomb waiting to explode. Because he feels so inadequate as a man, he tries to compensate by being even more obnoxious than the average high Air/Fire man. He has an abnormal need to demonstrate his "masculinity" at every given opportunity. He has to continually remind everyone that he is still a man, and therefore will invariably exhibit an excessive degree of overly masculine behavior.

This man will have a particularly touchy ego and does not appreciate a woman who dares to point out any of his areas of imperfection, especially when he has high Air emphasis. He can be quite paranoid about what he sees as criticism or a woman telling him what to do! The real irony here is that when these Air/Fire men are highly successful, they can still have real problems. Great success activates their male egos, and they see themselves as being really special. Certainly this man does not think that anyone, particularly a woman, should tell him anything!

There is, by the way, a great attraction to this combination of Air and Fire, the two most romantic Elements. This man's courtship behavior skills could create an emotional hurricane in your normal, organized existence—or, worse yet, in an abnormal, disorganized existence! This "gentleman" may keep you so preoccupied with candlelight dinners, flowers, gifts, and talk of his undying adoration that you may not have noticed that the two of you have never even discussed *you*. Well, he has probably made a few remarks about your life, perhaps in the way of helpful hints. The Elements of Air and Fire are so creative that these men can usually recommend a better way of doing almost anything. This would be a problem in itself, but, unfortunately, the aggressiveness produced by too much Air or Fire invariably causes their suggestions to have an overly assertive or opinionated tone. They tend to be very pushy about their recommendations.

An amazing thing about many high Air/Fire men is that, while they have a strong emphasis in the two most romantic

Elements, they do not necessarily use these energies. Their egos can be so enormous that they simply do not think they need to bother with the candlelight dinners and flowers in order to have women falling all over them. Or, with their Fire impulsiveness, they may have always jumped straight into relationships, never really stopping to "court" a woman. And if there is also major influence in the self-directed Eastern Hemisphere, such men might not concern themselves with the fact that women really like to be courted.

Very high Air/Fire also makes a man extremely judgmental. Together with his need for control of everything, this can be a truly charming combination! An exceptionally high Air/Fire man can be a sight to behold. He will not only make you nuts with his spoiled-child mentality and perfectionistic approach to everything, but may attempt to edit your communication and monitor your every action. With this type of chart, a man is virtually born spoiled. He would have needed a great deal of discipline as a child in order to have ever really grown up. These guys suffer from the illusion that the world revolves around their every wish.

Needless to say, no sane woman could possibly build emotional intimacy with a man (boy) who frequently wanders back to a more carefree time, acting like a preschooler in need of a nap. It is too bad that women are willing to remain in relationships with these men. The women who put up with this preposterous kind of treatment make these relationships possible by continuing to do so! Men like this cannot have relationships with women who have high self-esteem. If you are involved with this type of man, you simply must give up any thought that he will *ever* change; he will not and can not! This is his chart, this is who he is! Only if he had been strongly influenced and disciplined when he was very young, so that he entered adulthood without the typical Air/Fire "spoiled child" mentality, would a man with this kind of chart be an emotional grownup. (See Chapter 7: Is He an Emotional Grownup?) I doubt that you can find even a dozen men in the city where you live who have extremely high Air/Fire and who function emotionally as adults—who have emotional intelligence.

The irony here is that, since these guys are always looking for a better way of doing everything, one might think that they would take a long look at themselves and notice that there is some room for improvement there. Sadly, this is rarely the case. It seems that their masculine ego is so monumental, and they are so busy renovating and remodeling everyone else, that they just do not have the insight and awareness left over to direct at themselves. A woman with this imbalance might take a long look inward and then muster the motivation to change.

It can be difficult for a woman who is very Martian to find the right man. She needs a man who is very strong and confident. Most women would want this, but this woman really needs it. Regrettably, when a man has enough Martian in his chart to meet her needs, he will often be too overly masculine to be tolerable!

And unfortunately, when she does find him, he may have a problem with her Martian tendencies. He may not be appropriately appreciative regarding her creative (Fire/Air) ideas about how to improve the relationship!

But these men think that they already attract the "right" women, because for them, the "right" woman is simply one who will tolerate their commanding personality! There never seems to be a shortage of women who will endure being treated without respect in exchange for whatever perks the situation may offer, even if the only perk is to "have a relationship." Many women appear to have only one thing on their mandatory list: "he wants me!"

Due to their inability to change, it is impossible to build emotional intimacy with these men. Real intimacy involves responding to each other's need for change—adding or subtracting certain behaviors. (See Chapter 10: Why Some Men Find It Difficult to Tell You How They Feel for a full discussion of building emotional intimacy.) But one of the biggest problems here is that a man with this chauvinistic thinking will not allow himself to be told anything by a woman. He suffers from a deep-seated feeling that if he allowed a woman in any way to control or order him around, he would be a wimp rather than a man.

If you are in a relationship with a man like this, please get into a support group that will help you to get out and help you to see that you are a special person. You do not have to tolerate a man whose mere attitude toward you is an insult.

What women put up with such men? Interestingly, the ones most prone to do so are the flip side of the astrological coin on this gender issue. The women whose charts have too many planets in the feminine Signs of Earth and Water are the most likely candidates. A very high influence in these Elements causes an overabundance of the more passive, nonconfrontive traits. Women with such charts tend to have such a gentle, loving attitude that they find it difficult to assert themselves when dealing with overpowering, controlling men. If they have most of their planets in the feminine Signs, there will unfortunately be a lack of planets in the masculine Signs to provide them with the necessary confrontive and aggressive energies.

Now at least there is a way to avoid these men altogether! By understanding these astrological factors that invariably produce such Super-Martians, you can avoid becoming involved with this type of man in the first place.

It is desirable that any chart have a fairly even distribution of planets in the masculine and feminine Signs. Everyone, regardless of their sex, needs to have the capacity for caring and consideration for others, as well as for confrontive or even forceful behavior when required. Again, see Chapter 10: Why Some Men Find It Difficult to Tell You How They Feel for a full explanation of how the distribution of planets in the masculine or feminine Elements dictates whether a person will have a more passive or a more aggressive nature.

Will men who have only one or two Fire and/or Air planets necessarily have a major problem with overly masculine behavior? They may not exhibit a problem level of this behavior, but the traits will definitely be there at times.

Can a man with his Sun Sign in the feminine Element of Earth or Water have a problem with overly masculine behavior? Yes, most definitely! Certainly, if all of his other major planets are in Fire and/or Air, there will be very strong overly masculine behavior. However, even when there is only one major planet in Fire or Air, there can be a powerful influence, particularly with an isolated Fire Venus or Mars. While much will depend on his overall level of maturity, a man like this could be very determined in his point of view.

On the other hand, if all his major planets are in Fire and Air, and are in the Eastern Hemisphere (more self-functioning and less concerned with your needs), it very much increases the self-centered and controlling energies. (See Chapter 8: Men Who Are Hopelessly Self-Centered.) A man like this could be beyond help. You can pretty much forget about having a normal relationship with him. You will be lucky if you can have a normal conversation with him!

7

Is He an Emotional Grownup?

A man might possess the most compatible chart for you in all of Western civilization. But if he is not an emotional grownup, we do not care how wonderful his chart may be!

I certainly do not want to depress you any further regarding your efforts to find a decent available man. One would assume that you already view this as a rather dismal task! But whatever your other requirements may be, from financial status to hobbies in common, sometimes it seems as though nothing is as hard to come by as a man who is fundamentally emotionally mature.

There are planet placements in many charts that will interfere with an individual's ability to attain emotional maturity. This would obviously interfere with your ability to attain emotional intimacy with such a man.

Let's look at some of the chart imbalances that would indicate major emotional dysfunction. First, one of the most difficult chart factors for anyone to overcome: the man with high Air or Fire influence. (See Chapter 6: The Male Chauvinist, Astrologically Defined.) He may have terrific courtship skills, but there may be real problems lurking beneath his charming exterior. With Air and Fire being masculine Elements, this man will exhibit what I call "overly masculine" behavior: demanding, aggressive, opinionated, impatient, controlling, and judgmental. And invariably he will have a problem controlling anger.

Very few people understand how anger, and our inability to express it in a healthy manner, affects our lives in profoundly negative ways. The high Air/Fire men described above will often find it difficult to control their anger. The Elements of Air and Fire are very idealistic, perfectionistic, and impatient—not exactly a formula for the tolerance and acceptance that one needs in order to be considered mature.

Hemisphere Imbalance

Another way to determine whether someone is emotionally mature is to look at how they approach the all-important issue of self versus others. There needs to be a balance between looking out for oneself and concern for others. An emotionally healthy man will have a genuine ability to hear and care about your needs, attempting to meet them when it is realistic to do so without violating his most basic needs. In order for you to feel that you and your needs are of real interest to a man, he must have a balance of planets in the Eastern and Western Hemispheres in his chart. Individuals with extreme emphasis in either of these two Hemispheres can be very dysfunctional.

When a man is obsessed with meeting only his needs, when there is an abnormal level of emotional independence and self-centeredness, you will often find that the majority of his planets are in the Eastern Hemisphere (the Signs of Capricorn, Aquarius, Pisces, Aries, Taurus, and Gemini). These men are resistant to the concept of really needing anyone else emotionally.

On the other hand, when a man is so preoccupied with the needs and opinions of others that he consistently sets his own needs aside, we will undoubtedly find most of his planets in the Western Hemisphere (Sagittarius, Scorpio, Libra, Virgo, Leo, and Cancer). This influence, when it is extreme, produces individuals who are also potentially very insecure. They are so needy of others, so overly concerned with what people think of them, that they are deeply affected when the feedback is not positive.

When determining the level of dysfunction in terms of imbalance toward either Hemisphere, it is not just a matter of which Hemisphere his Sun Sign is found in; one must look at the other planets. Of particular importance are the three functional planets of Mercury, Venus, and Mars. (See Chapter 8: Men Who Are Hopelessly Self-Centered, for a complete look at the issue of Hemisphere balance.)

The Ultrasensitive High Water Man

Haven't we all known men who are ultrasensitive to emotional turmoil that they become upset and impatient that they cannot communicate in a mature way? This is one of my personal favorites! I was once involved with a gentleman whose exceptionally high Water influence prevented him from continuing a conversation in any normal fashion once he became upset. What is so ironic about high Water people is that, while they are extremely sensitive about what comes their way, they are unable to manifest any sensitivity about what goes out to others. They are so ultrasensitive that, when they get rattled, anxious, or uptight, your needs simply cease to exist for the moment. You will find this problem with men whose charts have three or more of the major planets in the Water Signs. And if there are also three or more major planets in the Fire Signs, good luck! You had better look for some extremely positive factors in his childhood—perhaps parents who were both therapists! A man with such a high degree of emotionality in his chart could theoretically be quite wonderful. But there would have to be many factors in the overall chart that would enable him to process this much emotion. Women will do much better with this type of chart, due to the fact that it has always been more acceptable for women to possess and show emotion. Fortunately, this is now gradually beginning to change; men now feel that they can come out of the closet emotionally.

Ego States

Another way of referring to an emotionally mature individual is to say that he is "adult ego state functioning." Dr. Thomas A. Harris wrote a valuable book on the subject of ego states, *I'm Okay, You're Okay*. The book does a masterful job of explaining normal and abnormal human functioning. Dr. Harris details the following ego states, which we all possess and function from on any given occasion: The Adult, The Vulnerable Child, The Joyous Child, The Spoiled Child, The Nurturing Parent, and The Critical Parent. A person's mental health can be evaluated by determining their functioning patterns in terms of these ego states. While an emotionally healthy individual will experience emotions and thoughts from all of the ego states, the adult ego state (our centered self) is the one from which we must function and make our decisions. Unfortunately, some people literally do not possess an adult ego state—at least not one in which they remain for any length of time, or from which they make their crucial life decisions!

Let us consider a man who is truly adult-ego-state functioning. Exactly how does that manifest in regard to his interacting with others? It will depend upon many factors in his chart, as well as what he was taught as a child and what he has learned along the way about thoughtfulness and generosity of spirit. But a man who is functioning from his adult ego state most of the time will have, at some point, made the critical decision that grownup people generally maintain a decent mood and a civil attitude toward others in the face of life's little annoyances. If this man has not learned to cope with life's unexpected rain showers, just imagine how much fun he will be during a real thunder and lightening storm!

When Is a Man an Emotional Grownup?

A man is no longer an emotional child when he has put the immature mentality of childhood behind him—the unrealistic de-

mands, the impatience, and the tantrums of a spoiled child. Individuals possessing true maturity have managed to develop
self-control and consideration for others as part of their instinctive behavior. A mature man does not put his urge to express childish frustration at a situation above the need to act in
a basically gracious and civilized manner, or above your need
to be treated decently. He does not allow annoyance or aggra-
vation to affect him to the degree that he loses sight of the
needs and feelings of the other individuals involved.

Please don't rationalize a man's rude or childlike behavior by
saying that he "had a bad day." We all have bad days! Real
grownups learn to deal with bad days. A man with emotional
maturity has learned to cope with his emotions, and has come
to accept an imperfect world filled with imperfect people.
When one of those less-than-perfect people does something
that causes him inconvenience, he is able to put that in perspective to see it as a part of life. He takes things in stride.

A man is obviously not an emotional grownup if he always
becomes angry and pouts when things do not go his way. You
must develop a habit of paying close attention to these enlight-
ening little warning signals. It would certainly be a major indication of the level of his problem if he showed any signs of this
type of behavior during the very early stages of your relationship. That is, after all, when he is supposedly impressing you
with his best version of himself!

I personally feel that a person's ability to maintain a sense of
humor at all cost is vitally important. He need not laugh out
loud in the face of annoyances, but hopefully he is able to
maintain some form of lighthearted or upbeat mentality in the
face of life's traumas. If nothing else, a person can always find
something absurd about a dilemma; if one cannot laugh at the
absurdities in this world, one is in big trouble!

The bottom line here is that all the astrological insight in the
world is not going to help you if you are willing to have a relationship with a man who is not an emotional grownup. An
emotionally mature woman would not have a friendship, much

less an intimate life-long partnership, with someone who has never graduated from the sixth grade emotionally.

When Will You Really Know Him?

You will really know him only after you have understood his astrological chart and spent enough time (months at the very least) interacting with him. How does he react in real life, not just during courtship? His chart will tell you a great deal more about him than just whether he is potentially compatible with you. The more balanced his overall chart (Elements, Hemispheres, Gender, and Modes), the less likely it is that he will be dysfunctional.

When beginning a friendship or romance with any man, do not make the mistake of presuming him to be emotionally mature—or even sane—until he proves himself to be so. To be on the safe side, one should presume that a man is not emotionally mature until he shows you otherwise. Do not become emotionally involved with a man until you really know him. It is impossible to really know anyone in a short period of time. (See Chapter 18: Somewhere Out There.)

I cannot tell you how many times I have heard my clients make the following unrealistic remark: "Even though I have only known him for a short time, I feel like I *really* know him." Right!! Two dates and, because of his exceptionally charming personality, terrific sense of humor, and desire to help feed the homeless (after all he did give that man on the street money for a Big Mac), an otherwise rational, sane woman suddenly feels as though she *really knows* a virtual stranger. It is utter nonsense! When a woman tells me, "Oh, but you don't know him—he's *so* wonderful," I remind her of the fact that *she* does not know him either, and that the only thing she knows for sure is that he *seems* wonderful! And when I hear, "I just know he's what he appears to be; I'd stake my life on it," that, of course, is precisely what one is doing these days! You must remember that there can be factors in a chart other than those which produce a delightful personality and outward demeanor.

This man with the positively scintillating personality could have chart factors that make him extremely self-centered, highly inflexible, and very demanding or controlling.

Any man you have only known briefly may be incredibly emotionally dysfunctional, with borderline sociopathic behavior that does not emerge until after you have allowed yourself to really care about him. His charming impersonation of a grownup may last until he maneuvers you into the bedroom. Then . . . presto! Pseudoman changes right in front of your eyes! Suddenly, he is not quite as concerned with your needs and desires as he had previously seemed. At worst, he could be anything from a self-centered pathological liar who failed to tell you that he has tested HIV-positive, to a true mental case whose violent side appears after he has a key to your condo.

I do not mean to sound like your mother, but after all of your less-than-fulfilling relationships (I feel safe in assuming this; it unfortunately applies to the majority of the population), maybe it is time someone stepped in with some handy hints as to how you can avoid relationships from hell!

Rule Number One is obviously to know a man for a period of time before you even think about allowing yourself to fall under his spell. If the magic hits you over the head from the first meeting, that's great, but put it in perspective. Tell yourself that *if* he "checks out" this could be very exciting. You would not buy a car without a test drive, so how can you become emotionally involved with a man without "test dates"? Hopefully, you would not accept a new job, no matter how great the company appeared to be, without interviewing your potential employer; you would ask the right questions to determine whether the job is really what it seems to be, and whether the company is offering the benefits that are important to you.

Dysfunctional Families

It is possible that a man with a normal, balanced chart could have had very imbalanced environmental influences that resulted in severe emotional and mental problems. It is imperative that you find out as much about his childhood as possible. You simply must avoid serious emotional involvement with men who had major negative childhood traumas.

Charles L. Whitfield, M.D., in his book, *Healing the Child Within: Discovery and Recovery for Adult Children of Dysfunctional Families,* tells us that 80 to 95 percent of all adults grew up in some sort of dysfunctional family. While virtually all families indulge in some form of dysfunctional behavior, real damage is done when children are not able to be themselves or to express their feelings. If this man was taught not to talk, not to trust, not to feel, he will bring these destructive habits, these patterns of survival, into every relationship. You are not his therapist. You cannot change the fact that he leads a life filled with depression, hurt, and anger.

Psychologists tell us that people who function in an emotionally healthy way in love relationships had fundamentally healthy interactions with their opposite-sex parent. It is extremely unlikely that any man who had a *really* negative and unhealthy relationship with his mother (not just one that lacked an ideal level of emotional rapport) will relate well with women in his adult life—particularly in a love relationship.

Love at First Sight

Probably one of the strongest indications of emotional immaturity is a habit of frequently "falling in love." Of course, in reality, there is no such thing as love at first sight. Instant attraction or lust, yes, but not love! Emotionally mature people realize that love has to involve liking as well as respecting the person. Needless to say, one cannot genuinely like, much less know enough to respect, someone one met ten minutes or even ten days ago. To really love someone, you must know a great deal about them, about their good and bad traits. I think that part of really loving someone is having affection for some of their less-than-perfect qualities.

Perhaps even more important than whether you can love someone you don't really know is the issue of whether you can feel genuinely loved by someone who does not really know you! In order to have the feeling of trust and security that are vital to a love relationship, you need to truly know that your mate sees you accurately and loves all parts of you. This is also a real boost to your self-esteem.

Of course, it is possible to be exceedingly attracted to someone you have not met at all—someone you see across the room—hence the term, "love at first sight" or, in fact, major attraction at first sight! I guess one should ideally "fall in like" first. When you initially like what you see a great deal, this could indeed be the beginning of "falling in love," but it should be a gradual process.

I am not saying that it is impossible for a mature man or woman to develop very strong feelings for someone in a short period of time. This might happen when someone is of an age when they have experienced many relationships, and is very attuned to the qualities needed in a mate.

When Does "I Love You" Mean Something Else?

When a man says "I love you" before he really knows who you are, he is actually only saying, "I love being with you," "I love your personality," "I love who I imagine you to be," or "I love the way you make me feel." After all, how can he love you when he does not yet know the whole you? It is a huge mistake to begin verbalizing the "L" word too quickly. This can throw both the "I love you-ee" and the "I love you-er" into the deep end of the pool before they are ready to swim. The person who blurts out such a serious term of endearment too readily may have problems living up to what he or she said if they haven't had the time to properly evaluate it. And the recipient of such early ardor may feel pressured by this statement, which may be perceived as, "I want to spend eternity with you!" A woman may wonder just how many other women this man has committed himself to so instantly.

When a man tells you that he loves you within a very short period of time, one has to wonder whether he possesses real emotional maturity. Is it simply the insecure or "child" part of him that wants to be in love? I urge you to suppress your desire to tell a man you barely know that you love him. If you have a strong urge to tell him how you feel, try something like, "I love being with you," or even, "I'm crazy about you," rather than, "I love you."

As adults, we ought to be able to make mature evaluations of our feelings, and realize that the new object of our affections should be viewed as a likely candidate for a mate and someone with whom we are very much interested in developing a relationship. While certainly a major attraction for someone can come out of left field, real love has to slowly take hold.

How Does He Deal with Emotions?

Now then, after you have established that the gentleman in question is not an escapee from a mental institution and is adult-functioning with an emotional age range somewhere near his chronological age, you might wish to consider whether he is able to get in touch with his emotions and process them in a healthy way. Does he confront his feelings and share them with you?

Confrontiveness is an extremely important factor in healthy relationships where people want to achieve true emotional intimacy. If everyone were capable of true confrontiveness, it would change the face of human relationships. As explained in Chapter 5: Why Can't a Man Be More Like a Woman?, it is the influence of the masculine Elements (Air and Fire) in our charts that produces confrontiveness. Those without enough Fire and Air influence in their charts find it particularly difficult to share their feelings.

One indication of a high level of emotional maturity is an ability to comfortably express both positive and negative emotions in a healthy manner. In other words, it is equally important for a man to be able to matter-of-factly tell you when he is unhappy with something, as it is for him to compliment you or share his joy and happiness with you. Unfortunately, most people seem to have a real problem with doing either of these things adequately, much less both of them.

Please do not think that you can change someone who is seriously emotionally dysfunctional. People (especially men) are often relatively content with their areas of dysfunction. They have learned over the years to adapt. They are simply inclined to seek out those who either do not notice their faults (however glaring they might be), or those who will overlook them. While overlooking another's relatively minor flaws and faults is what a healthy and realistic relationship is all about, ignoring blatant dysfunction is not healthy! A man who is 40 going on 12 emotionally is Mr. Wrong for *any* woman!

8

Men Who Are
Hopelessly Self-Centered

Why is it that some men appear to genuinely care about your needs, while others automatically put their own needs first? Wouldn't it be helpful to know if a man's chart (or for that matter, anyone's chart) matches your own in this important area—and to know whether the basic level of desire to connect within a relationship is fundamentally similar to your own? Well, now you are able to do exactly that!

It's in His Hemispheres

When evaluating chart compatibility, it is important to determine whether the majority of planets in a man's chart are located in the six Western-Hemisphere Signs (Sagittarius, Scorpio, Libra, Virgo, Leo, and Cancer), which are more relationship- and "other"-oriented, or in the Eastern-Hemisphere Signs (Capricorn, Aquarius, Pisces, Aries, Taurus, and Gemini), which are less relationship-oriented and more "self"-oriented.

Ideally, one would have an even distribution of major planets between these two Hemispheres. This produces a person who would instinctively put his or her own needs first in a healthy way when it is appropriate to do so, and yet be able to switch gears instantly to give the needs of another the consideration and attention required.

However, when most of the major planets are found in one of the Hemispheres, with no real influence from the other, a man will almost exclusively put either himself first (Eastern) or others first (Western) in an extreme way. These two types of men will differ greatly, not only in the way they respond within a relationship, but in their degree of need for relationship in the first place.

Important note: if you do not know the location of a man's other planets, you may simply read this chapter according to the Hemisphere of his Sun Sign. If the information seems accurate, then undoubtedly he has several major planets in the Hemisphere of his Sun. If, however, the description of the traits of that Hemisphere does not seem to apply to him, then it's possible that the chart has a good balance of planet influence in both Hemispheres.

This Hemisphere balance, as I have said, is extremely important in terms of a healthy approach to meeting one's own needs and the needs of another. One needs enough Eastern Hemisphere influence to provide a strong sense of independence and self-confidence so that one can make important life decisions and meet one's basic needs without fretting about what others will think. But one also needs enough major planet emphasis in the Western Hemisphere to provide a healthy approach to caring about and meeting the needs of others—to really hear and process the feelings and opinions of others.

But what if there is an imbalance between the Hemispheres? While an Eastern Hemisphere man usually manages to give you the feeling that his needs take precedence, the Western Hemisphere man could turn you off with his neediness and smother you with his undying love and attention. The Eastern Hemisphere man responds to others only after he has instinctively determined how the issue at hand will affect him. The Western Hemisphere man cares too much about your needs, and wants to help you so much that he will sacrifice too much and violate his own needs to meet yours. He is also inclined to be influenced by the opinions of others to the point of always changing his mind or his behavior to adapt to them.

In order for a person to achieve a healthy approach regarding his or her needs versus your needs, it is important for the chart to have the major planets distributed between the Western (others) and Eastern (self) Hemispheres. It is not the total number of planets that needs to be considered here, but the distribution of the major planets (Sun, Moon, Mercury, Venus, Mars, and Ascendant).

Extreme Hemisphere Imbalances

The following evaluation of extreme imbalances of the Hemispheres may sound exaggerated. However, if every major planet is located in one Hemisphere, the description of that Hemisphere will probably accurately describe the person's attitude toward self versus others. It is possible that very positive parental influences could produce an emotionally mature individual who would function in a more balanced manner in spite of very imbalanced Hemispheres. However, this would be rare and it would not alter the fact that a person's innate nature would tend to remain true to his or her instinctive Hemisphere. The strongly Eastern-Hemisphere-influenced man, even if he has developed the habit of stopping to give the needs of others more priority than he instinctively would, will still automatically process his own needs first in a split second. At this point, the evolved Eastern Hemisphere man would then be able to set his needs aside for another's when it is appropriate to do so. The strongly Western Hemisphere man, even though he has perhaps learned the importance of putting his needs first when it is appropriate to do so, will still innately think of the other party (feelings, needs, opinions, etc.) first in most instances.

Western Hemisphere Imbalance

In this case, the majority of the major planets in the chart are found in the Signs of Sagittarius, Scorpio, Libra, Virgo, Leo, and Cancer. Such a Western Hemisphere person would be very incompatible with an Eastern Hemisphere person, who could not begin to relate to this level of relationship neediness.

Given a choice between a man with an imbalance in the Eastern or the Western Hemispheres, it would probably be better for him to be too Western. Being male, he will already have a dose of the more masculine type of Eastern traits. Incidentally, since the Western Hemisphere traits tend to be more feminine in nature, a woman with a Western Hemisphere imbalance would tend to be even more extreme than the description that follows.

The man with too many planets in the Western Hemisphere tends to be insecure and lacking in self-confidence. This will be particularly true if he has no significant influence in the Eastern Hemisphere, which is so important in terms of providing a sense of self and independence. He will be overly concerned with what others think of him. This man will probably get many opinions before making decisions of any consequence. Even after making up his mind, he may change it if others do not seem to approve.

This is the nice guy who lets friends take advantage of him, and who does not know how to say "no." He may lend money to people who never pay him back, and do favors for those who are never there for him. These men may not complain about how they are treated, because they may not notice it themselves; part of being the nice guy is to always make excuses for everybody. As my sister-in-law once said about the extremely Western Hemisphere type of individual, "If you're tired of being used as a doormat, stop lying down in front of the door!" But bear in mind that the instincts are so strong in these people—the urge to please and to do things for others—that you may as well tell a cat not to chase a mouse!

Just think of the Western Hemisphere man as the exact opposite of the self-functioning, emotionally independent, Eastern Hemisphere man who almost seems not to need anyone, and it will help you understand the incredible difference between these Hemispheres. Regardless of all other chart factors, including the exact Signs or Elements involved, nothing else spells out so clearly an individual's very need for relationships and his capacity for making you feel that you are important to him on a day-in-day-out basis as does his Hemisphere balance. The Western Hemisphere man will apologize if he steps on his cat, whereas the Eastern man may not apologize for stepping on *you!*

But while a man with too much Western Hemisphere could make you feel very wanted and needed, he could also make you nuts with his excessive attention and his need for your constant show of love. What you have here is a relationship junkie. He really does need all that frequent feedback from you in order to feel good about himself. When both parties are Western Hemisphere relationship junkies, both people will be tripping over themselves to meet each other's needs. Lord knows when either person would find time for much else!

If you are very Eastern Hemisphere, you could crush this poor man with your need for independence. You might get annoyed with him if he asks why you didn't call him when your meeting ran longer than anticipated. He is sincerely hurt because he would have broken away from a meeting to call you; that's what Western Hemisphere people do. While any person ought to make such a call out of consideration, it is the Western Hemisphere person who will be especially crushed when he doesn't receive such a call.

I am convinced that codependents are simply individuals with all or most of their major planets in the Western Hemisphere. As surely as Eastern is too independent, Western is too codependent. They can expend so much effort in their involvement with the lives of others that they simply do not have enough energy left for themselves.

Eastern Hemisphere Imbalance
In this case, the majority of the major planets are found in the Signs of Capricorn, Aquarius, Pisces, Aries, Taurus, and Gemini.

An adult-functioning individual with an Eastern Hemisphere imbalance could be very compatible and happy with someone whose chart also had strong Eastern Hemisphere influence. They might both be too preoccupied with their own needs to notice or care whether the other party is paying attention to their needs. And yet, oddly enough, because highly Eastern people are so into their own needs, the one area in which they can be quite aware of you is in terms of whether you are able to respond to their needs as much as they do!

Incidentally, a woman with too much Eastern Hemisphere influence in her chart will typically not be as extreme as a man in terms of self-centeredness and lack of giving to others; her feminine traits can offset these tendencies. However, a woman with this chart imbalance is likely to have relationship problems as a result of not responding to her mate's needs and feelings.

As far as having a relationship with an overly Eastern man, if your chart does not have a similar influence in the Eastern Hemisphere, it had better be balanced at least between Eastern and Western Hemispheres. If your chart is strongly Western Hemisphere, you would undoubtedly be negatively affected by this man, whose instinctive ways could devastate you with his lack of response to your needs.

By the way, this one can appear very appealing during courtship behavior days. Finally, a man who is independent, a man who is not constantly worrying about what everybody else thinks! How refreshing, how challenging—this man will not bore you to death by always doing everything you want him to do! However, you may soon realize that you cannot get him to do *anything* you'd like him to do. It would be rare for him to ever do something for someone without having first dissected and analyzed the precise effect it would have on him (and he can do this instinctively in a split second).

As another indication of their level of obsessive independence, Eastern Hemisphere men will rarely turn to others for help, even family members and intimates. They need to do it themselves! They do not want to feel obligated to anyone! Accepting help might mean they would be expected to return the favor someday, and they might find that inconvenient; it might get in the way of some need of theirs that would then go unfulfilled!

If you are a Western Hemisphere woman who sincerely wants to help a totally Eastern Hemisphere man overcome a problem, you may become very frustrated in your efforts. He will invariably end up feeling that you are trying to control him—that you are somehow invading his space.

The extreme Eastern man's pride in his independence can make it impossible for him to comprehend that someone could ask another for help except in the most dire circumstances—and maybe not even then!

The vast difference is that the Eastern chart is not really comfortable needing others or being needed—certainly not in the way the Western chart does. For example, just yesterday my Aquarian niece with major Eastern Hemisphere influence said to me, "I need *not* to need anyone!" This could be the credo of the Eastern Hemisphere mentality.

It's not that these individuals are cold or unloving per se. It is not that they do not care about others at all. They just operate on a different wavelength when it comes to their needs versus the needs of others. Eastern Hemisphere men are just so incredibly independent in their very nature that it would be hard for them to ever give you the feeling that you are really needed to begin with. They are so fundamentally self-oriented, so organically involved in their own needs, desires, hopes, dreams, and wishes that they don't have a great deal of time or energy left over for anyone else's desires or dreams.

When it comes to respecting, or even really hearing, your opinions, Eastern Hemisphere men can have great difficulty. They are just so involved with their own opinions, which may automatically discount yours, that they cannot step outside themselves long enough to genuinely process yours. It is really quite a phenomenon. You can explain all of this to them—they can even read this chapter—and they will not necessarily understand or agree. Their opinion will probably be that this does not apply to them; it simply sounds too negative, thereby conflicting with their view of themselves. Naturally, there will be times when your opinions do not conflict with theirs—when they will be able to genuinely listen and respond in a positive way.

When a man has some influence in the Western Hemisphere (perhaps one major planet or two or three outer ones) it can actually be rather crazymaking. He will momentarily hear, understand, and care about your feelings, but will often go right back to acting (or should I say, *not* acting) through his Eastern influence.

It can be difficult to achieve genuine emotional intimacy with a man who is massively Eastern Hemisphere. If he also has high masculine influence (planets in Air and Fire), it will be especially difficult for him to hear and respond to your needs enough for you to feel the degree of affection that is necessary for real intimacy. (See Chapter 10 for the definition of building emotional intimacy.)

The chart factor that would most contribute to a man with Eastern Hemisphere influences being even more self-centered would be a high masculine influence. If, God forbid, he had all of his major planets in the masculine Elements of Fire or Air, you would not want to know this man! He could truly redefine selfishness! Any man with extremely strong emphasis in the masculine Elements of Air and Fire is already going to possess many traits similar to those of the self-centered Eastern Hemisphere man. (See Chapter 6: The Male Chauvinist, Astrologically Defined; this chapter will give you an understanding of how these men with too much masculine energy react in intimate relationships.) A combination of high masculine and Eastern Hemisphere influences could explain sociopaths! These guys have a great deal of difficulty perceiving that you even *have* needs or feelings, much less responding to them (particularly when they conflict with their own).

Let me elaborate for a moment. These men may relate to your *having* feelings, but often only as it relates to *them*. In other words, they can identify with your feelings of happiness when they do something for you that they are in the mood to do, or to your joy when they buy you a gift that *they* want to buy you, at a time when *they* want to buy it. They are fundamentally aware of the fact that you have feelings; it's just a tricky concept for them that your feelings have anywhere near the importance or validity that theirs have. Whereas the Western Hemisphere man can usually easily put himself in another's position, the Eastern Hemisphere man finds it almost impossible to genuinely understand or sympathize with anything that he himself would not do, think, or feel.

A man like this may initially seem quite normal indeed. He may have a very pleasant personality and sophisticated courtship skills that could carry him for the first few weeks. But his profound self-involvement is such that although you may know that he loves being with you, loves showing you off, loves the way you make him feel, loves being in a relationship, you will never really feel that he loves *you*.

If you look for warning signals, you will undoubtedly find them in the first phone conversation, and certainly on the first date! You will notice that he talks a great deal about himself, and that he seems to have a remarkable lack of interest in you. He will not ask you questions about yourself. When he does, it will only be to ascertain information about you as it applies to him. Do you like his car? Do you like the snow? (*He* has a cabin in the mountains.) Do you like Italian food? (*He* makes the world's greatest lasagna.) When you do get the floor for a moment and talk about something of interest to you, he will look for the first opportunity to jump in and get the conversation back to his favorite subject: himself! Invariably, this will happen without his bothering to take up valuable time by commenting on anything that you have just said.

You will finally begin to get the idea that you, and anything in your life, are just not very interesting to him. You will find that when you introduce him to someone of importance in your life, there will be nothing from him in the way of normal feedback. He will probably not even bother to muster up a simple, "Your mother is very nice." And you will notice very little in the way of sincere response to what you are saying. There will be relatively few comments pertaining to you. He will tend not to make even the simplest remarks of a personal or supportive nature, such as, "Oh, that sounds great," "Good for you, I'm glad you told her how you felt," "You must feel terrific about that," "I'm sorry you're so disappointed," and so on. By the way, if he is also a Thinking Sun Sign, the odds are even slimmer that you will ever hear these types of emotionally reassuring comments.

If you are thinking that his inability to converse in this manner is not crucial, think again. One of the most important things we can feel from someone we love is that they are genuinely concerned about us, about how we feel, and about how the world is treating us. How can you feel that concern from a person who doesn't bother to make the most obvious remarks about something in your life that you are sharing with him?

There are some highly Eastern Hemisphere men whose overall chart influences reflect a very caring and considerate nature, and who have managed to achieve a high degree of emotional maturity. Such men will be exceptions to the level of self-orientation described here.

Note: Maybe there is a need for *independency* groups to teach Eastern Hemisphere people how to be more considerate of others and more relating! However, something tells me that there would not be a waiting list of Eastern people who were just dying to learn how to be more sensitive to the needs of others.

Are Extreme Hemisphere Influences Always Obvious?

Not always. There are many instances in which a man's Hemisphere energies will be affected by childhood influences. For instance, when life influences have been extreme enough to produce an Eastern Hemisphere man who is insecure and needy, he may indeed be quite codependent. This way of functioning will present even greater problems and stress for him than it would for the Western Hemisphere man, for whom this degree of dependence comes more naturally. This Eastern man will work against himself. While his needs may be great, his being so Eastern will interfere with his ability to give enough to receive what he wants in return.

Other factors in a chart may make a person with major Eastern emphasis seem more Western. Planets in both the romantic Fire Sign of Aries and the Water Sign of Pisces can often make a person (especially a woman) much more relationship-oriented than the average Eastern-Hemisphere person. However, this individual, in spite of being almost a "relationship junkie," will still be very Eastern Hemisphere in their basic way of functioning.

Now, when a man with most of his major planets in the Western Hemisphere is functioning from a spoiled-child ego state, he may be so unrealistic about what to expect from others that he can be very selfish and demanding in attempting to meet his extreme needs. While he can appear Eastern in personality, he is classic Western in his neediness, this being the very thing that caused him to have become Scrooge-like as a result of feeling hurt and rejected by others. This would be particularly true if he has a strong masculine influence (planets in Fire or Air). This produces real anger and impatience with others when his needs are thwarted.

The Clash of the Hemispheres

A clash of Hemispheres frequently spells relationship disaster. It can present constant problems if you do not understand and accept the totally different way in which your mate deals with his needs as opposed to your needs. While there may be a few rare cases in which two adult-functioning, evolved people do not have a major problem with this clash (although even these couples will relate to the dynamics described here), the following description depicts the typical behavior and attitude patterns of people with opposite Hemisphere influence.

THE ZODIAC

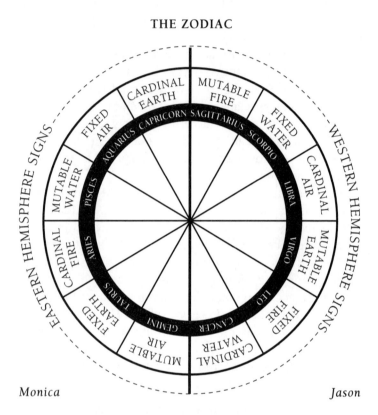

Monica   Jason

The Influence of Eastern and Western Hemispheres

The number of planets that one has in the more "self-oriented" Eastern Hemisphere versus the more "others-oriented" Western Hemisphere will have a major influence on the role that other people play in our lives. This will affect everything from our innate ability to look at things from another's point of view to our willingness to do things for others.

The worst Hemisphere clash will be between a woman who has the majority of her planets in the Western Hemisphere (others are very important) and a man with most of his planets in the Eastern Hemisphere (the focus is more on self). She will always need more than he can give; he will see her as too demanding and too needy.

JASON (Western Hemisphere)

Sun:	Scorpio
Moon:	Virgo
Mercury:	Sagittarius
Venus:	Scorpio
Mars:	Leo
Jupiter:	Pisces
Saturn:	Aquarius
Uranus:	Leo
Neptune:	Scorpio
Pluto:	Virgo
Ascending:	Cancer

MONICA (Eastern Hemisphere)

Sun:	Pisces
Moon:	Taurus
Mercury:	Pisces
Venus:	Aries
Mars:	Taurus
Jupiter:	Scorpio
Saturn:	Taurus
Uranus:	Libra
Neptune:	Sagittarius
Pluto:	Virgo
Ascending:	Capricorn

Let's look at a couple who have such an extreme clash, with the woman having virtually every major planet in the Eastern Hemisphere, and the man having all but two planets in the Western Hemisphere. The astrological wheel (facing page) illustrates this major Hemisphere clash between Jason (Western influence) and Monica (Eastern influence).

Jason will appear very codependent, behaving like a "relationship junkie" in terms of his neediness and his desire to connect with Monica. He may have a need to "possess" and control her. It will be difficult for him to feel sufficiently loved and appreciated by her, even though she may sincerely love him, because she will not relate to him in a way that will allow him to perceive her as being faithful and devoted.

This is due to Monica's very autonomous attitude. Her whole persona, her very being, is one of independence and self sufficiency. Jason does not want her to be too self-reliant. He needs to be needed. He will never feel that she needs him enough. On the other hand, she needs to be independent and needs her space. Jason is crushed by her need for space; it makes him feel rejected and unloved. He is also going to feel very insecure as a result of her independent personality. Monica will seem elusive to him—always just "out of reach." He will feel jealous without any concrete reason. He may even subconsciously feel that she must be needing some other man in the way that he needs her. He cannot imagine that this level of need, which is like breathing to him, is nonexistent in her.

The exact opposite is true for Monica. She needs her space, and therefore feels that anyone who really loves her will understand that and respect this need. Jason's need to possess and control her makes her feel trapped and smothered. And around it goes. Jason and Monica will be forever mismatched when it comes to this issue of self versus others.

In order for a couple with these opposite Hemisphere needs to have a healthy relationship, there would have to be many other very positive chart factors to offset this particularly difficult area of incompatibility. It would help a great deal for them to fully understand this Hemisphere clash. They would also need to be dedicated to developing the habit of responding to the other party's very different needs.

9

Is He a Natural-Born Couch Potato?

Does he take initiative? Does he follow through? Is he flexible? Why is Aries so filled with energy for new projects? Why is Taurus so set in his ways? And why is Pisces always changing his mind? Aries is the Fire Sign with the most initiative. Taurus is the most stubborn of the Earth Signs. Pisces is the Water Sign with the greatest flexibility. But why?

One of the major factors that determines the differences between Signs of the same Element is something called the "Mode." The Mode is the channel through which the Element operates. It is indicative of how the Element will manifest its energy in that particular Sign, in terms of initiating things, persevering and following through, or being flexible and adaptable.

How the Modes Affect Behavior

There are three Modes: Cardinal, Fixed, and Mutable. There are four Signs in each Mode. The distribution of Modes in a chart is crucial to how the individual functions in life: Cardinal gets things started, Fixed has the drive to keep things going, and Mutable is open-minded and has the ability to adapt to new input.

It is highly advantageous to have an even distribution of the Modes in one's chart. This is an enormous help in terms of allowing one to successfully pursue life's opportunities in a

TABLE 9.1   THE MODES, THEIR QUALITIES, AND THEIR SIGNS

CARDINAL SIGNS (initiative, energy, stamina, control)
Aries
Cancer
Libra
Capricorn

FIXED SIGNS (determination, perseverance, drive)
Taurus
Leo
Scorpio
Aquarius

MUTABLE SIGNS (flexibility, adaptability,
                              open-mindedness)
Gemini
Virgo
Sagittarius
Pisces

---

healthy and balanced fashion. Many problems can result from serious Mode imbalances.

If you are a parent whose child has a Mode imbalance, it is extremely important that you help that child to adjust his or her energies accordingly. This could make a real difference in later life, creating more productive early patterns than those that would have developed naturally.

Let's look at the these Mode influences to see how drastically people's basic functioning and relationship interactions are affected by the distribution of Modes in their chart.

The Cardinal Mode

Balanced Cardinal Influence

With two or three major planets in the Cardinal Signs, a man will have a solid Cardinal emphasis, which is very attractive to women. We want a man who does things, who has goals, and who attacks life with vigor and vitality. This man, since he is always thinking of things to do, will be more inclined to return phone calls, buy you gifts or flowers, and even run those thankless errands. This type of man will seem to be holding up his end of the relationship. We all know how important that is! This is the man who will make dinner reservations and get theater tickets to a show that you've been hinting you want to see, unlike a low Cardinal man, with whom you have to play "relationship secretary"!

High Cardinal Influence
With most of the major planets in the Cardinal Signs, this person would have enormous initiative to go forth eagerly and begin new projects with great enthusiasm. Such people have a profound desire to make things happen, to change things. They are the movers and shakers. They have a tremendous urge to *do things*—to set things in motion! There is a real need for a sense of accomplishment. When there is too much Cardinal influence, not only will a person probably be jumping from one project or crazy scheme to another, but there may not be the capacity to see things through to completion (that is where the Fixed Mode comes into the picture). And if the capacity for completion is there, there might not be enough Mutable emphasis to afford flexibility and allow a change of direction when required.

The most classic representation of Cardinal energy is found in the Sign of Aries. How many times do we see Aries people coming up with new and better ways to do everything—wonderful new projects to jump into—and then nothing ever comes of it? This would not be the case, of course, with every Aries individual—only the ones who have several other planets in Aries or the other Cardinal Signs. When there is very high Cardinal influence, there is a real need for at least one major planet in a Fixed Sign, in order for there to be a prayer of follow-through on some of these projects. Very high Cardinal men are also extremely controlling, and if such a man has a

Thinking Sun Sign, he is going to be a master at controlling his emotions. We will not see much spontaneous, unedited expression of his feelings!

Note to parents: the high Cardinal child must be encouraged in every way possible to finish every new project. This is not to say that they must always finish every single thing, but if your child is constantly starting things and never following through, there is a real problem that you will need to address. Encourage your child to slow down and think before jumping in with both feet. It would be a good idea to get a commitment up front that certain projects will be completed. This child will also want to run the show; don't let him or her boss friends around!

Low Cardinal Influence

Those without major planets in the Cardinal Signs will tend to lack the desire to make things happen. Such a man may have great talent and ability, but he may not have a strong urge to put forth the effort required to be successful, whether in business or in his personal life. This type of man will be exceptionally frustrating when it comes to working on relationship problems. With low Cardinal influence, he will simply not possess that desire to change something or to make an impact. Such individuals tend to "let life happen to them" rather than making things happen. It's not that he doesn't want to see the relationship improve, it's not that he doesn't think that he will participate. You may share all of your wonderful insights, brilliant ideas, and well-thought-out plans, and he may share your enthusiasm, but he will then proceed to behave in the same old ways. This will be particularly true if his Venus (how he loves) and his Mars (how he acts) are in Fixed Signs. If these two planets are in Mutable Signs, and if his interest in the relationship is very strong, he may indeed initially respond to your ideas and react to your energy, but he still will not really seem to "be at the other end of the relationship." You will not have the feeling that he is a partner in the project.

Those with low Cardinal influence will also tend to lack energy or stamina, may tire easily, and tend to need more rest than those with higher Cardinal influence. They would also lack initiative and the incentive or ability to challenge others or circumstances. (See high Fixed and high Mutable; these individuals would definitely be high in one or both of these Modes, and have the problems of these imbalances.)

Note to parents: low Cardinal children will need to be encouraged to find projects that will capture their imagination. Urge them to *do* things! And make sure that such a child gets enough rest. When the Cardinal emphasis is very low, there tends to be less stamina than normal.

The Fixed Mode

Balanced Fixed Influence
With two or three planets in the Fixed Signs, a man will have follow-through on projects and an ability to persevere in the face of adversity. He will be open-minded and not be so stuck in his own point of view that he ignores every outside influence and goes forth at all cost, unlike a man with a majority of planets in the Fixed Signs.

High Fixed Influence
With more than three major planets in the Fixed Signs, a man would have a strong sense of conviction and be very attached to his own point of view, possessing a great ability to persevere at all cost. The Fixed Signs of Taurus and Scorpio have even more drive and determination than the other Fixed Signs of Aquarius and Leo. A man with extremely high Fixed influence could be difficult to live with, being very bent on having his way. Probably the most aggravating thing about people with this imbalance is their inability to change or to alter any behavior. What you see is what you get!

It is therefore difficult for extremely high Fixed men to develop true emotional intimacy with anyone. The very definition of this kind of closeness depends upon one's ability to hear the other party's needs and desires, and to adapt accordingly. (See Chapter 10: Why Some Men Find It Difficult to Tell You How They Feel.)

A man with high Fixed influence can be so set in his ways that he finds it very difficult to change behaviors. When highly motivated, he may succeed in adding something positive to his repertoire (particularly during courtship), but it is unlikely that he will be able to eliminate anything negative.

If, heaven forbid, all of his major planets are Fixed, you can pretty much kiss your thoughts goodbye of him ever changing anything! One cannot just look at the total number of planets in the Fixed Signs. There is a particularly strong influence when we are looking at functional planets being in Fixed Signs. A man can have very good Mutable emphasis with his Sun, Moon, and even perhaps Mercury (the brain) in the Mutable Signs. But with the other two functional planets of Venus and Mars in Fixed Signs, he will be very fixed in his feelings and actions. He can be extremely set in his ways in terms of how he acts (Mars) and how he expresses love (Venus).

Note to parents: a child with extremely high Fixed influence absolutely must be taught at a very early age about the importance of being flexible and remaining open to the ideas and opinions of others. A young child with this very difficult imbalance can learn to develop the habit of flexibility! The fact that someone is born with an exceedingly strong instinct does not mean that the situation cannot be significantly altered with behavior modification.

Low Fixed Influence
When there are no major planets in the Fixed Signs, there can be a real problem with the ability to follow through on anything. With the resulting strong Cardinal and Mutable emphasis, there will be loads of initiative to start projects and flexibility to change direction when necessary, but very little drive to stick with anything and make it happen (see high Cardinal and high Mutable).

Note to parents: this particular Mode imbalance can be greatly helped by encouraging children to finish what they start.

The Mutable Mode

Balanced Mutable Influence

With two or three major planets in the Mutable Signs, this man will tend to be flexible in his outlook, and open to hearing another point of view. Even if other chart factors cause him to be strong-minded or give him a tendency to be self-centered, you will be able to reach him through his planets in the Mutable Signs (particularly if his Mutable involves the functional planets).

High Mutable Influence

With most planets in the Mutable Signs, a man would simply be so changeable, so overly flexible, that indecision would prevail; it's always "back to the drawing board." He would have real difficulty making up his mind and sticking to it, always finding reasons to reconsider everything. The capacity for "possibility thinking" is endless. If he also has too little Cardinal influence, there would be a lack of desire to begin projects or to implement plans. With this combination, you wouldn't want to get too excited by any ideas this man has, because he might change his mind before anything came of it anyway.

Note to parents: high-Mutable-influence children very much need to learn to make good decisions and stick with them. They desperately need to develop self-discipline. This particular Mode imbalance can be helped a great deal by solid parental guidance.

Low Mutable Influence

Having few planets in the Mutable Signs produces an individual who is not flexible or adaptable. Such a person won't feel comfortable with any type of change.

A man with this imbalance would be difficult to communicate with and very frustrating. He is obviously going to have either high Cardinal or high Fixed influence, or both (see above). He would be very inflexible, opinionated, and controlling. Solid Mutable emphasis is necessary in order for a man to have the ability to analyze things from a point of view other than his own. Even if he had high Air influence to give perspective and objectivity, he would not have the innate urge to adapt and change, either for your sake or his own.

Note to parents: children with this imbalance have a real need for parental guidance. They must be constantly encouraged to be more open-minded, more flexible, and more attuned to the needs and feelings of others.

As you can see, a balanced Mode influence is exceptionally important in terms of how a man's energy manifests in life in general and certainly in his relationships. Does he have ambition and the urge to accomplish (Cardinal)? Will there be the perseverance and determination and drive to realize his goals (Fixed)? Will he be flexible and able to readily change his mind when necessary (Mutable)?

10

Why Some Men Find It Difficult to Tell You How They Feel

Don't you love it when the man you have been seeing for three years informs you one day that not only does he not adore your special guacamole dip (though he's managed to impersonate someone who loves it on numerous occasions), but that he is not even crazy about avocado? A simple question comes to mind: "Why have you been keeping this deep dark secret?" The answer is invariably, "I didn't want to upset you." Now, of course you are not the least bit upset that he has been faking his pleasure all this time!

What is it that prevents people from telling it like it is? How many times have we all failed to participate in full disclosure, perhaps on matters even more relevant than guacamole dip? Why do so many people function in this way, avoiding telling others their true feelings and needs? Because many individuals are too Venusian, having too many planets located in the non-confrontive Signs of Earth and Water. Chapter 5: Why Can't a Man Be More Like a Woman? explores in detail the importance of a chart being balanced in terms of planets in the Martian and Venusian Signs.

The Martian Signs Are Instinctively Confrontive

Fire:	Aries-Leo-Sagittarius
Air:	Gemini-Libra-Aquarius

The Venusian Signs Are Instinctively Nonconfrontive

Water:	Cancer-Scorpio-Pisces
Earth:	Taurus-Virgo-Capricorn

Individuals whose charts have a strong influence in the confrontive Martian Signs of Air and Fire have a greater innate urge to express their needs—to let you know who they are, how they feel, and what they think. The man with this type of chart would be more inclined to let you know when he does not like something, and to compliment you on something he does like.

A lack of confrontiveness is probably the single greatest cause of problems in human relationships. The inability to share one's true needs and feelings creates difficulties in any type of relationship, but certainly in one where you wish to feel true emotional closeness. How can you feel really emotionally connected to a man if you do not even know how he feels, if he does not know how you feel? When there are too many planets in the feminine Elements, it can have a negative effect in every type of relationship.

Some people are so nonconfrontive that it is not even a question of them not telling you how they feel; many times they do not know themselves! One must start with confronting one's own feelings before they can be shared with another. It is extremely important to develop the habit of constantly asking ourselves what our true needs and desires are in any given situation.

The following description of what's involved in creating true emotional intimacy explains how mandatory it is to let those close to us know exactly what's going on. The depth of intimacy achieved between any two people will be a direct result of how successful they are in really hearing, caring about, and responding to the needs of the other party. They must be willing to tell each other, "This is what I like, and this is what I don't like," whenever appropriate. The degree to which they are both able to hear and respond to each other is directly correlated to the level of real emotional intimacy that they are capable of achieving. Obviously, neither party will reach anything close to 100 percent, in terms of either adding desired behavior, or subtracting undesired behavior. It is simply a matter of knowing that your mate genuinely cares about what you need and that he will sincerely attempt to meet those needs, without violating his own needs in an unhealthy manner. In essence, this is what creates a feeling of true affection for another person. This formula applies to any type of close relationship, not just a romantic one.

Unfortunately, many men and women are hesitant to let their partners know what they like or don't like in a relationship. By sharing the things that bother them, many people feel as though they are being too critical or demanding. How many mothers have said to their children, "If you can't say anything nice, then don't say anything at all!" Even telling their mate what they like or need can cause overly Venusian people to feel guilty; they think that the other person might interpret this as too pushy or controlling. There is also the basic fear that if you tell someone who you really are, they will not like you any more. People develop the habit of not sharing their deepest feelings with others, for fear of being ridiculed or perhaps even abandoned.

People who have astrological charts with a very strong influence in the nonconfrontive feminine Signs of Water and Earth can have a very hard time learning to share their thoughts and needs. This is not to say that they never do so, it is just a matter of what energies people come by naturally. How instinctive is it for them to readily share their feelings, to bare their soul to another?

If you look at a man's chart to determine how comfortable he might be regarding sharing his feelings, you will want to look at the number of planets in Fire and Air. You also must know which planets are involved. The following three planets will affect an individual the most in this area: Venus (how he loves), Mars (how he acts), and Mercury (how he thinks). I put the "brain" of the chart last on this list because people are so often inclined to proceed based on "love" and their urge to "act," rather than on what they "think."

If all three of these planets are in Water or Earth, a man will have difficulty in consistently expressing himself in a confrontive manner (especially with a Water Venus; this guy will withhold just about anything in order to not hurt your feelings!). On the other hand, if all three are in the masculine Signs of Fire or Air, he will innately be more inclined to share his feelings and needs.

There are a couple of other factors that can produce an individual who is naturally communicative. The exact placement of Mercury and Venus is very important. When these two planets, which influence communication, are found in the same Sign, there is a powerful urge to talk about one's feelings. These people are very verbal—almost too much so in many cases. They simply have a natural desire to tell (Mercury) you how they feel (Venus).

It is crucial that a couple be totally honest and completely open with each other. You want to know that if your mate occasionally comes across in a manner that is cool or aloof (and if there is even one major planet in Air, it is a given), it has nothing to do with something brewing inside of him regarding you. You don't want to wonder whether he failed to tell you about something at the time when it happened, and now the emotion is about to come out in an area unrelated to the original issue. (Are you as crazy about passive-aggressive behavior as I am?) In other words, if you need (and don't we all?) to feel secure, to really trust a man, how is that remotely possible if you do not believe that he will virtually always tell you about his thoughts and feelings that pertain to you—to the two of you?

This habit of nonconfrontiveness is truly destructive to all relationships. Fortunately, like any other habit, the habit of not sharing one's needs and feelings is something that can be changed (though usually with great difficulty). One of the most important benefits of always knowing, and letting others know, where you stand is that it helps reduce stress.

The Emotional *versus* the Mental Elements

Fire and Water People: Feeling Has Priority

11

The Feeling Sign Women: Fire and Water

THE FIRE SIGN WOMEN: ARIES, LEO, SAGITTARIUS

FIRE TYPE OF EMOTION: Dynamic, Confrontive, Impulsive, Enthusiastic, Passionate, Perfectionistic, Futuristic, Idealistic, Romantic, Confident.

GENDER: Masculine (Martian, confrontive).

More direct and outspoken than the feminine Elements of Water and Earth.

Emotionally compatible with Water and Fire Sign men.

As a Fire Sign woman, you are an extremely independent lady with a fiery and passionate nature—very romantic and idealistic, possessing great confidence and enthusiasm for life and all of its unlimited possibilities!

You need a special kind of man who can meet your strong need for romance—to be wined, dined, swept off your feet, worshipped, and adored! Yet somehow he must manage to give you the vague lingering impression that he is not putty in your hands. Now that, you must admit, is very tricky—quite a balancing act! Need you wonder why you have had such a hard time finding

Mr. Right? Incidentally, if you also have Venus in your Fire Sun, your need for the romantic grand gesture and a dynamic, demonstrative show of love will be even greater. Fire thrives on excitement; a relationship absolutely must be exciting if it is to last!

The problem side of all this Fire energy is a tendency to jump into relationships too quickly, becoming emotionally involved before you really know a man. (See Chapter 7: Is He an Emotional Grownup?) Unfortunately, those of you who also have more than two additional planets in the Fire Signs can readily succumb to your fiery urge to "act at all cost"—even when you know that it would be foolish to proceed!

There is a big payoff for Fire people in learning to slow down, consider the ramifications, and look before you leap. Developing the ability to control your emotions and postpone pleasure can result in great joy and satisfaction. For the Fire person, anticipation is in itself very exciting, and Fire thrives on excitement. You might as well at least enjoy that part of the situation, since it may often surpass the encounter itself. Sometimes planning the party can be more fun than the party!

The positive side of this Fire zest for life is that it makes you an emotional survivor. When relationships end in disaster (and, unfortunately, many of those impulsive encounters do just that), you bounce back more readily than the other Elements. Being goal-oriented, with an abundance of hope and optimism, you are right back in the game. That bounce-back aptitude comes in handy for Fire individuals who persist in entering into relationships with less information than one would insist upon when buying a used car!

I am by no means scolding all of you Fire ladies for this impulsive approach to love. Some of you have observed, along the road of life, that things work out better with a bit of self-restraint and moderation. And there are those of you who have the good fortune to have an overall balance of Elements, making you a little more rational about the whole matter.

Now let us take a look at the kind of man with whom you ought to be contemplating involvement. One's own Element is technically the best for potential emotional compatibility. Fire Sign men will have your romantic soul and share your brand of passion for life and love. You will appreciate each other's spontaneity and impulsiveness.

However, if his overall Fire influence is too high, there can be some problems with his being too Martian (see Chapter 6: The Male Chauvinist, Astrologically Defined).

Because of the possibility of this overly masculine behavior in Fire men, I tend to prefer Water Sign men (Cancer, Scorpio, Pisces) for Fire women, provided that they have enough Fire elsewhere in their charts. These men are ultrasensitive and at times may need to be handled with kid gloves. These men are often drawn to the Fire woman's fiery qualities, but a Water Sign man will need a major planet or two in Fire in order to relate to a Fire woman's intensity.

As far as Earth (Taurus, Virgo, Capricorn) and Air (Gemini, Libra, Aquarius) men are concerned, they are a definite no-no for the Fire woman (see Chapter 3). Their extreme mental nature is a major clash with your emotional nature. I assure you that, no matter how attracted you may be to one of these men, in the long run there is a vast difference between the two of you in how you handle emotion. He is unable to truly comprehend your deepest emotional nature. He will think you are too intensely emotional, always talking about how you feel. You will see him as too emotionally distant or too logical and realistic about everything.

By the way, it is important that your man be supremely confident—certainly enough to match your self-assured personality! It takes a man with a strong sense of self to give you all of the space and independence that you require. Of course, he must also be exceedingly sensitive and emotionally responsive, with plenty of patience to offset your Fire impatience (another reason why Water men are sometimes better for you than Fire men). Naturally, he must possess a major dose of generosity; otherwise, he may not surprise you with all of those little impromptu gifts and baubles that Fire women require. And, finally, he absolutely must be spontaneous and impulsive so that there will be no risk of you ever becoming bored!

I apologize for spelling out so clearly all of the qualities that almost every Fire woman needs desperately. But what else could I do? I'm an honest Sagittarius. Besides, I knew that, being a Fire Sign woman, you would rise above it and accept the challenge that Somewhere Out There (see Chapter 18) is such a man—and, yes, in this galaxy!

The Aries Woman: Fire Feeling Sign
(March 20–April 20)

ELEMENT: Fire (a bold, dynamic type of emotion).

Enthusiastic, Idealistic, Ambitious, Impulsive, Romantic, Courageous, Adventurous.

GENDER: Masculine (Martian, confrontive).
May be too confrontive with others, possibly without enough sensitivity for their feelings, particularly if you have several planets in Fire or Air Signs.

EASTERN HEMISPHERE: Less relationship-oriented than Sagittarius and Leo; less preoccupied with the needs of others than Western Hemisphere Signs.

A CARDINAL SIGN: Energetic and ambitious.

Emotionally compatible with Water and Fire Sign Men.

Aries is the adventurer and leader of the zodiac. You like to take the lead in love, particularly if you have additional planets in Aries. It's a difficult situation, because you would be horribly bored with any man who succumbed to your every need and granted your every wish. And yet, you certainly do not relate to anyone going to the other extreme and thinking that he is going to run the show.

Aries women are terribly intrigued by men who do not seem all that taken by their charms. (Aries, being a Cardinal Sign, loves a challenge!).

While all Fire women need exceptional men—they seem to require men who have it all—it can be especially hard for Ms. Aries to find Mr. Right. Being the most idealistic of the Fire ladies, you may be too quick to judge whether a man matches your vision of the perfect lover. Please don't rule men out too quickly simply because they don't initially appear to meet your every criteria! Be more flexible in your evaluation process.

I am not worried about you hanging on to a negative relationship. Of all the twelve Signs, Aries is the most aggressively independent, the least likely to put up with a situation he or she finds undesirable. To begin with, an Aries woman is less in need of a man than the other Signs, and if someone treats you badly, you are out! (If you have Venus in Pisces, you will unfortunately be inclined to hang on to an unhappy situation longer; Water Venus finds it difficult to leave relationships.)

Aries, even more than the other Fire Sign ladies, virtually must have a man with a strong Fire influence. You have an extreme need for a knight in shining armor; your man must be brave and courageous and very romantic—he has to be your hero!

Let's look at the Fire Sign men who share the passion in your heart and the romance in your soul. Sagittarius, the most flexible and fun-loving of the Fire Signs, is my first choice. The Leo man, though he really likes having things his own way, can be terrific. He is very confident, loyal, and devoted. A fellow Aries could work if he has a balanced chart (I would really like to see him with Venus in Pisces). Aries men can be really impossible in terms of overly masculine behavior, though one with the right chart could be fantastic!

Because of the problem that these Martian Fire Sign men have with overly masculine behavior, the best match for an Aries woman is sometimes a Water Sign man (Cancer, Scorpio, Pisces). Ideally, he really ought to have a Fire influence in his chart. This would allow him to better identify with your fiery nature. The ultrasensitive Pisces man might have planets next door in your Sign of Aries, which increases compatibility. Cancer is the most emotionally responsive of all the Signs, and he will share your Cardinal energy. Like Aries, Cancer is a Cardinal Sign—courageous, and loving of challenge. Scorpio, with his great willpower and determination, can be very attractive to Aries women.

The Thinking Elements of Air (Gemini, Libra, Aquarius) and Earth (Taurus, Virgo, Capricorn) must be ruled out entirely for you emotionally intense Fire Sign women! The absolute worst match of all would be Virgo, the Sign least like Aries in the entire zodiac. A Virgo, being the sensitive Thinker with his gentle ways and touchiness to criticism, could be tromped on by the exuberant emotional nature of Aries. If you are involved with an emotionally reserved Earth Sign man, do not allow this man to convince you that you are at fault for being the way you are. I remember a client whose Virgo husband had virtually convinced his Fire Sign wife that anyone with her brand of fiery emotionality simply had to be certifiable!

When you do find that right match for you, do not ruin it all by being so independent that he doesn't feel the least bit needed, or by overdoing the Aries tendency to always point out a better way of doing everything. It is amazing how few men appreciate women who consistently point out the errors of their ways. With all that Fire creativity, surely you can find a way of subtly slipping in the really pertinent helpful hints.

The Leo Woman: Fire Feeling Sign *(July 24–August 23)*

ELEMENT: Fire (a bold, dynamic type of emotion).

Enthusiastic, Idealistic, Perfectionistic, Loyal, Proud, Noble, Creative, Romantic, Regal, Magnanimous.

GENDER: Masculine (Martian, confrontive).

WESTERN HEMISPHERE

A FIXED SIGN: Determined and persistent.

Emotionally compatible only with Water and Fire Sign men .

Leo—Queen of the jungle! If your man does not make you feel worshipped and adored—and, perhaps equally important, appreciated and respected—he had better start packing! Though you would never really be a happy kitty without total adoration, you would be utterly miserable without respect and appreciation. Not that all the Martian Signs don't need to feel these things, but for you it is mandatory! Your knight in shining armor had better also excel in the flexibility and understanding departments, because he is going to have to live with the fact that you like to do most things according to your blueprints.

It is not that you just "like" to do things your way, it is part of the very Leo nature! Your Fire independence precludes any man from demanding that things be done his way. You may run across an occasional Leo lady who will allow the man in her life to have things his way. She will have Venus in Cancer.

The Leo woman is potentially most compatible with her own Element of Fire. These Fire Sign men are passionate, dynamic, emotionally expressive, honest, and romantic. The best of the Fire Sign men for a Leo lioness would probably be the generous and enthusiastic Sagittarius. The adaptability of this Mutable Sign would help to balance your determined Fixed traits. Aries and Leo could be a terrific but challenging match. However, with you both being rather strong individuals, this one could be entitled, "Who's the Boss?" As far as a Leo man is concerned, it can be an excellent match (if the overall charts are good) once you two figure out the roles of "worshipor" and "worshipee."

Due to the problem that so many Fire Sign men have with overly Martian behavior, a Water Sign man (Cancer, Scorpio, Pisces) is sometimes a better match for a Leo woman. Of the Water Sign men, the one I prefer is Cancer. Along with your Sign of Leo, Cancer is one of the most devoted of all the Signs. Being an ambitious Cardinal Sign, Cancer has the drive and energy that you find so necessary in order for you to respect a man.

Earth (Taurus, Virgo, Capricorn) and Air (Gemini, Libra, Aquarius) men must be ruled out! (See Chapter 3.) It is impossible for a Leo woman to achieve real emotional intimacy with the Mental Sign men. They are of another emotional galaxy for Fire and Water Sign women. Earth and Air men tend to become anxious when expected to express their feelings in the manner needed by a Fire Sign woman. They will perceive you as being too intense, too emotional. You will view the Thinking Sign men as too emotionally cautious and reserved. A Leo should make a point of avoiding the two Fixed Mental Signs of Taurus and Aquarius.

Possibly the most important advice I could give a Leo woman would be to view the potential partner in your life with as much objectivity and flexibility as possible. Attempt not to judge men through those idealistic Fire-colored glasses, and, when you find the right man, do not always insist on things being your way. This may or may not be a problem with your particular chart, but do be on the lookout for it.

A final note: please remember that if a man does not appear to be obsessed with your every wish and need, it does not mean that he does not love you dearly or that he is not the right man for you. (Okay, he needs to obsess a little bit!)

The Sagittarius Woman: Fire Feeling Sign
(November 23–December 21)

ELEMENT: Fire (a bold, dynamic type of emotion).

Enthusiastic, Idealistic, Goal-Oriented, Impulsive, Creative, Romantic, Humanitarian.

GENDER: Masculine (Martian, confrontive).

WESTERN HEMISPHERE

A MUTABLE SIGN: Flexible and changeable.

Emotionally compatible only with Water and Fire Sign men.

Sagittarius is the friendly puppy dog of the zodiac. You must have a man who responds to that, who appreciates your effervescent personality! Fire is the most emotional of the four Elements, and with this Sign being the most enthusiastic of the Fire Signs, a Sagittarian woman might just overwhelm a man without enough Fire emphasis in his chart!

Sagittarius, being the "seeker of the truth" and the philosopher of the zodiac, requires that a man be sincere and honest to a fault. You certainly need a man who is psychologically minded and growth-oriented. Some might tell you that a Sagittarius woman must have a man who is very athletic and sports-minded, since the typical Sagittarian lady is the physical, outdoor type. While this may often be the case, it certainly depends upon the rest of the chart influences. Many Sagittarian females are fundamentally more relationship-oriented than athletic-minded. Recreation-oriented though you may be, often this may amount to playing a friendly game of tennis with your lover on a romantic weekend getaway. If he is the right man for you emotionally, you may not care if your only mutual recreational endeavor is an occasional stroll on the beach!

You need a man with whom you can not only have an emotionally rewarding relationship, but who can talk about it, and who is always looking to improve it. Because you are the most outspoken of the Fire Signs, any man with whom you are seriously considering a relationship must be open-minded and receptive to your input. You don't need overly touchy men who are ultrasensitive to what they might interpret as criticism. It is simply your Sagittarius nature to help others by sharing your ideas and insights. You need a man who is as interested as you are in finding ways to forever enhance the relationship. Not all Sagittarian women will possess this urge to an extreme, but if you do, you certainly need a man who can fully appreciate your unique and enthusiastic Sagittarius energy.

A Fire Sign woman definitely needs a man whose approach to love is intense and dynamic—a man capable of grand romantic gestures. That man will be a Fire Sign man! They are passionate, intense, and dynamic.

A fellow Sagittarius would be the best of the Fire Sign men. His zest for life is unequaled by any other Sign. However, he had better be old enough to have grown up a little; these men seem to take longer to mature than most. This guy needs to have reached a point where he has dated enough women to have gotten it out of his system, or you may as well make an appointment to see him in a few years after he has done so. The Leo man is also potentially a good choice. This dynamic and exciting man is also very devoted to friends and family. Bear in mind, though, that a Leo man really likes to have things his way. He needs major planets in the Mutable Signs to balance out his Fixed influence. And, finally, the energetic and adventurous Aries man! He needs to be emotionally mature, and should preferably have an overall balanced chart to help reduce some of his strong Martian tendencies.

Now, what about the gentle, caring Water Sign men (Cancer, Scorpio, Pisces)? Due to the fact that many Fire men exhibit overly masculine behavior, Water Sign men are sometimes my preference for Fire Sign women. However, the Water man would ideally have Fire in his chart to offset the Water brand of ultrasensitivity.

Which of the Water Signs would be best for Sagittarius? Cancer would be my first choice. They are ambitious, protective, and the most emotionally responsive of the zodiac. Scorpio would be my second choice. These men are the most emotional of all the Signs. You will be intrigued by Scorpio's mysterious side. The emotional wavelength between you will be enhanced if he has planets in Sagittarius. A Pisces man with a good chart that includes major planets in the Western Hemisphere could also be a good match.

Earth (Taurus, Virgo, Capricorn) and Air (Gemini, Libra, Aquarius) men are both highly emotionally incompatible with Fire women (see Chapter 3). They are on totally different emotional wavelengths. You will not be able to really *feel* their love. There is a lack of emotional responsiveness. These men are fundamentally uncomfortable with too much emotional display, whether negative or positive. You are a Sagittarius; need I say more?

There is one thing that Sagittarians really have to watch out for, with their penchant for being completely honest. People can be hurt or offended by the absolute truth, particularly the typical Sagittarius sarcastic version of it. Sagittarians are not known for their subtle approach, but rather for a certain innocent bluntness. You know, a lack of brutal honesty is not necessarily dishonest. It is a matter of discretion. So when the man of your dreams asks you if you think he is as sexy as Mel Gibson, do not tell him in the name of honesty that, while you think he is very sexy, he reminds you more of Woody Allen! Since most Sagittarians have become rather adept at social recovery, you'll breeze through the remainder of the evening explaining to him how humor is incredibly sexy, and how you have had a crush on Woody Allen since you were twelve!

Being a Sagittarius, you are a true humanitarian at heart; you may be on some kind of crusade to save the world, or at least rescue some of its underdogs. Most Sagittarians are real "animal people." Your Mr. Right may not be out there with you setting up pet orphanages or shelters for the homeless, but he'd better understand your need to do it.

Even with all that Fire self-assurance, you still have a very strong need to feel loved. And since, oddly enough, this very confident Sign of Sagittarius is possibly the most sensitive to rejection of all the Signs, you had better team up with a man who is capable of making you really *feel* his love for you.

Many men could love you dearly, but you need one who can make you feel it. Heaven knows you will be capable of making him feel it! When a Sagittarius woman is really in love with a man, no other Sign of the zodiac has your incredible capacity to demonstrate your love with such genuine concern and passion!

THE WATER SIGN WOMEN: CANCER, SCORPIO, PISCES

WATER TYPE OF EMOTION: Gentle, Extremely Sensitive, Kind, Sympathetic, Compassionate, Understanding, Forgiving. More gentle and sensitive than the other Feeling Element, Fire.

Emotionally compatible only with Water and Fire men.

GENDER: Feminine (Venusian, nonconfrontive).

Water Sign women are exceptionally loving, caring, benevolent, and deeply concerned with the feelings and needs of others. The Element of Water is very creative and intuitive and the most emotionally sensitive of the zodiac. The Water Signs of Cancer and Scorpio, being in the Western Hemisphere, are especially prone to caring too much, giving too much to others, and not doing enough for themselves. When a chart has every major planet in the Western Hemisphere, it is difficult for a Cancer or Scorpio woman to find any time for living her own life; she is preoccupied with helping others and solving everyone else's problems. A woman with this chart imbalance needs to focus on being more protective of her own needs, goals, and desires. (See Chapter 5: Why Can't a Man Be More Like a Woman?)

Another problem area for Water is a lack of confrontiveness. This may be the single greatest cause of negativity in relationships. In Chapter 10: Why Some Men Find It Difficult to Tell You How They Feel, you will find my description of how to build emotional intimacy, which depends upon both individuals being able to tell each other what they like, as well as what they do not like. It is critical to the success of a relationship and to one's emotional well-being to be open and honest about needs and feelings. The fact that it is difficult for a Water Sign person to do so can actually be blamed on one of Water's finest attributes. The very essence of your loving concern for others is what can prevent you from letting them know when something bothers you. You cannot stand to hurt anyone's feelings! It is so ironic that this very thing can end up causing such pain and hurt for others and yourself as well.

With enough planets in Fire or Air in your chart, you will be more comfortable with confrontation, more able to express your wants and needs. These two masculine, and therefore confrontive, Elements give an individual the urge to express his or her thoughts and feelings. However, the average Water Sign person really needs to work at becoming more outspoken and direct. You need to look out for *you!*

While the best emotional compatibility for a woman of any Element will be with her own Element, this is exceptionally true of the Water Sign woman. You really need a Water Sign man. He will be on your ultrasensitive emotional wavelength. This man will share your need for a type of emotional closeness that tends to be foreign to the other Elements. However, the other emotional Element of Fire is also potentially compatible. As you do, he gives emotion priority over facts and thoughts.

But remember, Fire is a different type of emotion than Water. Fire is a type of bold, intense, dynamic emotion. While Water is Venusian emotion, Fire is Martian emotion. Therefore, it would be ideal for a Fire Sign man to have a major planet or two in your Element of Water. This will help him to relate to your Venusian type of emotion.

What about the Earth and Air men for Water Sign women? These men are a no-no! Mental Sign men clash with Emotional Sign women. You will be unable to achieve true emotional intimacy with an Earth or Air Sign man. These men are a disaster for Water women in terms of real emotional compatibility. They are fundamentally uncomfortable with emotions, and are apt to give the impression of *thinking* their feelings, rather than *feeling* them. You may, unfortunately, be drawn to Air men due to their sensitive nature, but you must bear in mind that their sensitivity manifests in a very different way than yours. Yours is an emotional sensitivity, theirs is a mental sensitivity. There may appear to be great similarity, until you look more carefully. Water Sign women really need an in-depth understanding of Air Sign men in order to see the pitfalls. Because these men can be so thoughtful, considerate, and pleasant, they may remind you of the sensitive Water Sign men. But there is a *tremendous* difference between these Elements. Do not be confused simply because he may be adept at verbal communication and therefore manages to make you believe that he really loves you (and he may indeed). This is not the issue. How will he go about expressing his love to you? How will he react under stress? You need far more emotional responsiveness than an Air Sign man will be able to give you on a daily basis.

It is extremely important that any man with whom you become seriously involved be highly sensitive and very protective of you, both emotionally and financially. Emotional babies are not for you. Avoid like the plague any man who displays frequent emotional outbursts or temper tantrums! This is where things become very frustrating; the Water Sign men with whom you share such emotional similarity, and with whom you belong, are often not emotionally stable enough, hence the reason that many of you lean toward Earth Sign men who will provide the sense of security that you need. This is unfortunate, because these men will never be on your emotional wavelength, and will never really understand you. What you need is a Water Sign man, ideally with enough planets in the Earth Signs to ground him in reality.

When you do become involved with a man who you know in your heart is wrong for you, exit before you become emotionally attached; the Element of Water develops attachments more readily than any other Element. It can be particularly difficult for a Water Sign woman (especially if your Venus is also in Water) to break off a relationship. You simply are too loving, too forgiving, and too understanding—sometimes to a very negative degree, forgiving men for the unforgivable! One of the difficulties here is that Water is just so sensitive to the pain that others feel, that you certainly do not want to be the cause of it. The Element of Water has a real problem with the emotion of guilt. If a relationship is negative and needs to be ended, it is not your fault simply because you are the one to have the awareness and courage to bring it about.

And always remember: as a Water Sign lady, with your soft-hearted, gentle soul, you will only feel safe and build true emotional intimacy with a man who always treats you with concern and consideration and makes you really feel loved. This, almost without exception, will be a Water Sign man.

The Cancer Woman: Water Feeling Sign
(June 22–July 23)

ELEMENT: Water (a loving, gentle, nurturing brand of emotion).

Benevolent, Sympathetic, Forgiving, Compassionate, Sentimental.

GENDER: Feminine (Venusian, nonconfrontive).

WESTERN HEMISPHERE

A CARDINAL SIGN: Energetic and ambitious.

Emotionally compatible only with Water and Fire Sign men.

Cancer is the sentimental lady of the zodiac. She is exceptionally nostalgic, sometimes holding on to things long after they have served their purpose. You are by far the most sensitive of the Water Signs. Cancer women can have a real problem with insecurity. It takes the regular use of Martian energy to feel confidence and self-esteem. With Cancer being the most Venusian Sign of all, there is a real need for enough Martian (particularly major planets in Fire) in your chart to give you more confidence.

You are extremely aware of the feelings and needs of your loved ones, and can be deeply crushed when they are not equally attuned to your needs. The type of man who will call you in the middle of a busy day just to tell you how much he cares about you is not just nice for a Cancer woman—it's virtually mandatory! There is a real need for a man to demonstrate affection and shower you with frequent terms of endearment.

And a man must be very protective of you. Being a Cancer, you are very protective toward those you love. It is only natural that you would have a need to feel the protectiveness of the man you love.

With Cancer having such a deep brand of emotionality, it is extremely important that you make every attempt to define all of your needs and feelings, and then share them with anyone in your life with whom you hope to develop emotional intimacy. One of the problems unique to the Sign of Cancer is the fact that the crab will often move sideways and backwards when its actual goal is to move forward. Cancer individuals will often be unaware of their own goals and motives, assuming that if they are in a reverse mode, then it must mean they want to move backward. This is a reasonable enough assumption with any other Sign, but often not the case with Cancer.

Cancer is a Cardinal Sign, which means that you possess ambition, energy, stamina, and strength of character as a balance to your great sensitivity. The four Cardinal Signs are all very intense and powerful. Being a Water Sign, Cancer does not appear as dynamic as the other Cardinal Signs, but I assure you that it is; you just have a shy, or even sly, way of presenting it. The four Cardinal Signs are all very dynamic and powerful. While Cardinal Fire (Aries) and Cardinal Earth (Capricorn) exhibit this power more readily in their personalities, Libra and Cancer often fool people with their gentle Air or Water demeanor, which hides the intense Cardinal force just under the surface—"steel in a velvet glove!" Perhaps men are so taken by Cancer women because they are so charmed by the shy, demure quality, and so drawn to their inner strength.

All Cardinal Sign women need men who are ambitious. He may not yet be financially secure, but he had better be working on it. Lazy or uninspired men are not for you!

Water Sign men are the most likely candidates for understanding and relating to your level of deep emotionality because they operate on the same extremely loving wavelength. Your own Sign of Cancer is your best match. You will have your mutual Cardinal energy and ambition in common. You will also share the quality of emotional responsiveness and a protective nature. And you both love home and family; Cancer men and women can make wonderful parents. However, if you both retreat into your shells at the same time, I do not know which one will coax the other out.

Scorpio would be my second choice for you; you are both Western Hemisphere Signs, and therefore have a strong need for relationship and emotional bonding.

And the Pisces man, though he may drive you a little nuts with his changeability, is a kind, gentle soul. (See Chapter 8: Men Who Are Hopelessly Self-Centered, in order to fully understand the Pisces man's more self-oriented side.)

The other Feeling Element of Fire would also be potentially emotionally compatible. But he must have enough Water in his chart to produce a Venusian brand of emotion to offset the "overly masculine" behavior problem that Fire Sign men can have.

Hoping that we are talking about a Fire Sign man with Water influence in his chart, let's look at the individual Fire Signs. Leo, being in the same part of the wheel as Cancer (Northwestern Hemisphere; most devoted to family) would be the best choice of the Fire Signs for you. However, this being a Fixed Sign, these men really like to have things their way. Don't let him go overboard with that Leo "King of the Jungle" thing. Sagittarius could be a good match since it is the most flexible (Mutable) of the Fire Signs. However, not all Sagittarius men can provide the feeling of emotional security you need. Aries is the most Martian of the Fire Signs and can be difficult without a balanced chart. An Aries man can be very exciting; he is the most bold, dynamic, and adventurous man of the zodiac.

Regarding your emotional compatibility with Libra or Capricorn, despite the fact that you share Cardinal strength there is very little potential for building true emotional intimacy with any of the Air or Earth Signs (see Chapter 3: The Clash Between Thinkers and Feelers). These men are on a totally different wavelength when it comes to their level of comfort with emotion. They think first, and then feel. You, on the other hand, generally feel first and then think. Incidentally, while you may feel that Air Sign men seem very sensitive, do not mistake this mental brand of sensitivity for the brand of emotionally sensitive relating that you require. Their sensitivity will manifest in being very touchy to what they view as your being critical or controlling of them—whereupon they can become distant and removed! The degree of this Air tendency will depend upon how many major planets a man has in the Air Signs.

A final note: please do not make the mistake of remaining with a man who doesn't deserve you. This is a common habit for Cancer women. It is particularly common if you have Venus, the planet that determines how you approach love relationships, also in Cancer. The passivity of Water and the protective nurturing instincts of Cancer contribute to your potential inability to extricate yourself from a miserable and hopeless relationship. This inability to leave a negative situation will be further underscored if you also have several major planets in the Western Hemisphere. I am certain that Western-Hemisphere-imbalanced charts make up a high percentage of codependency group membership. Be good to yourself and get out if you know that it is the only solution! Cancer women are probably more miserable than most when they feel trapped in an unhappy relationship. Find a man who will really appreciate you!

The Scorpio Woman: Water Feeling Sign (October 24–November 22)

ELEMENT: Water (a loving, gentle, nurturing type of emotion).

Intuitive, Secretive, Intriguing, Determined, Obsessive, Intense.

GENDER: Feminine (Venusian, nonconfrontive).

WESTERN HEMISPHERE: More relationship-oriented, more concerned with the needs of others.

A FIXED SIGN: Determined and persistent.

Emotionally compatible only with Water and Fire Sign men.

Scorpio is the mystery lady of the zodiac. There is a truly magnetic quality to your personality, which cannot help but attract throngs of men. Fortunately, your extremely perceptive intuitive qualities, bordering on the psychic, can be of help in sorting out the phonies and the unworthy. Given the almost mystical charm and powers of Scorpio, you might have your choice of the remaining contenders. When things do not go smoothly in a relationship, you have the courage and tremendous willpower to work things out (hopefully you are attempting to do so with a man who is astrologically compatible). And, if you have planets next door in the goal-oriented Fire Sign of Sagittarius, it could make for a very determined approach to love. Unquestionably, Scorpio possesses the greatest emotional intensity of all the twelve Signs. And Scorpio possesses a seriousness second only to Capricorn. Scorpio, ruled by Pluto, the planet of obsession and compulsion, produces an individual who is rarely lukewarm about anything; everything in life, both good and bad, will be viewed through the eyes of intense passion!

Speaking of eyes, there is something in the eyes of a Scorpio that reveals the smoldering passion within. With Scorpio being a Fixed Sign, you have to make every attempt to avoid becoming so "Fixed" on the object of your obsession that you lose perspective and all ability to review the situation objectively. All Fixed Sun Sign individuals benefit a great deal from having at least two major planets in the Mutable (flexible) Signs to help offset the inflexibility of their Sun Sign. If you have Mercury (the brain of the chart) next door in the analytical Air Sign of Libra, that would help add perspective and objectivity to your thinking process. Incidentally, if your Venus (the planet that determines your approach to love relationships) is also in Scorpio, this will further heighten your intensely emotional nature.

What kind of man could begin to handle all this obsessive passion? Only a man with a similar brand of passion! And, equally important, a similar brand of emotional sensitivity: a fellow Water Sign. While I recommend that anyone is potentially more compatible with someone of their own Element, this is especially important for Water Sign women. Your unique level of ultrasensitivity virtually requires that a man be a Water Sign in order to fully understand your deepest feelings and to be capable of responding to those feelings, which will make you feel genuinely understood, and, therefore, loved. Water Sign men possess a special ability to relate to you on your emotional wavelength. These men can be wonderful. Some of them can be very difficult. Some of them can be wonderful one minute and difficult the next!

Now let's take a look at the Water Sign men. As far as your own Sign of Scorpio, with positive composite charts, this could be good. However, there can be problems with two Fixed-Sign people in a relationship. Because you are both so nonconfrontive by nature, you may never tell each other anything. I tend to prefer Cancer men for Scorpio women. They are usually good providers (Cardinal ambition), more protective than the other Water Signs, and the most benevolent of all the Signs. Pisces men, if you find one with an overall balanced chart, could be fine. But do watch out for the ones with the typical Pisces problems: being a flexible Mutable Sign can make Pisces men too indecisive and changeable. And they are Eastern Hemisphere, making them less concerned with the needs of others than either Scorpio or Cancer.

The only other Element to consider is Fire—the other Feeling Element. But Fire Martian emotion is very different from the Venusian emotion of Water. Fire expresses a brand of outgoing, dynamic, confrontive emotion that can make Water people uncomfortable. But with a Fire Sign man whose chart reflects a balance of Elements and solid Water influence, there could be excellent compatibility.

The best choice among the Fire Sign men for a Scorpio woman would be the Mutable Sign of Sagittarius. Since Sagittarius is next to Scorpio, this offers the possibility of his having planets in your Sign, and vice versa. Leo, being a Fixed Sign like Scorpio, would certainly need major planets in the Mutable Signs. The remaining

Fire Sign of Aries is dynamic and adventurous, but he is Eastern Hemisphere, and therefore not as concerned with your needs as the other Fire Signs. The exception to this will be the Aries man with strong Western Hemisphere influence.

You must rule out all of the Thinking Signs (Earth and Air). These men tend to think first, and then feel. They are cut of a *very* different emotional cloth than you (see Chapter 3: The Clash Between Thinkers and Feelers). They will not ever really understand your Water brand of sensitivity. Read Chapter 14 on the Thinking Sign men so that you may more fully understand the clash between Water women and these men, who almost have an allergy to feeling or showing too much emotion.

You may, however, find yourself attracted to Air Sign men due to the fact that they have a very sensitive nature. However, because their brand of sensitivity is more mental, it manifests very differently than Water. And, unfortunately, they are often much more sensitive about what comes *their* way than they are about what they send *your* way! When an Air Sign man has several major planets in the masculine Elements of Air or Fire, he will have the same overly masculine problems as the Fire Sign man. He will then be very touchy about anything he perceives as criticism, and can turn cold and distant in a heartbeat when he becomes upset or anxiety-ridden. Often, all it may take to upset him is a mere suggestion on your part as to how the relationship could be improved. He will perceive this as your trying to control him, and with high Air influence, *he* is the one who wishes to be in control of everything!

There are some Scorpio traits that could cause problems within a relationship. First, Scorpios often have too much Western Hemisphere influence. If so, you undoubtedly do too much for others. I would guess that the majority of people in codependency groups have an abundance of planets in the Western Hemisphere. And Scorpio is the most Venusian, the most nonconfrontive Sign of the zodiac. Unless you have functional planets (Mercury, Venus, Mars) in the confrontive masculine Elements of Fire or Air, you will feel quite uncomfortable with confrontation. With Scorpio having such depth of emotion, you often do not even know what you are feeling, much less whether you will be able to share it with another. Also, there is a certain secretive Scorpio quality; you will never share all of your thoughts and feelings with anyone. Non-confrontiveness is probably responsible for more relationship problems than any other single factor. Scorpios have to work hard to combat this natural instinct against exploring their deepest feelings. Develop the habit of telling people how you feel and what you need! This is a key ingredient in your own sense of well-being as well as in relationship happiness for Scorpio.

The Pisces Woman: Water Feeling Sign
(February 19–March 20)

ELEMENT: Water (a loving, gentle, nurturing type of emotion).

Understanding, Sympathetic, Forgiving, Compassionate, Sentimental, Intuitive, Perceptive.

GENDER: Feminine (Venusian, nonconfrontive).

EASTERN HEMISPHERE

A MUTABLE SIGN: Flexible and changeable.

Emotionally compatible only with Water and Fire Sign men.

Pisces, will you ever find the man of your dreams? Well, that may depend on whether you are willing to give up one of Pisces' worst habits: being so forgiving and understanding that you return time and time again to relationships that should be ended so that you can pursue something positive!

You really must stop doing this. How can you possibly find even "Mr. Right for Now" if you are continually willing to associate with "Mr. Wrong for Anybody"—a man who doesn't even deserve a date with you, much less a relationship! Unfortunately, one of the most wonderful Pisces qualities—of not being able to bear seeing a living creature in pain—can be so obsessive that it may become your worst trait. It is ironic that Water Sign women show such concern about causing pain to someone who has caused *them* nothing but pain! And, since Pisces has a tendency to procrastinate, you will be inclined to put off the inevitable: ending a relationship that you know is bad for you.

Another problem, in terms of being involved with the wrong men, stems from the fact that the planet Neptune rules Pisces. Neptune's influence produces illusion and delusion, often causing confusion when it comes to judging the men in your life. In many cases, you may conveniently overlook major negative traits. I can picture a Pisces woman saying with full sincerity, after having seen her lover in a restaurant with his female cousin, "Well, okay so he wasn't home keeping his sick cousin company; it's probably because she was feeling better and there wasn't any food at home, and he was nice enough to take her out to get some nourishment. I'm sure he wasn't stroking her face; he was probably just feeling her forehead to see if she still had a fever." Now, we really must learn to view life with a bit more perspective and realism!

It takes a special man with great sensitivity to fulfill the emotional needs of the gentle Pisces lady. It would be difficult for anyone but a Water Sign man to either fully understand or sincerely relate to your ultrasensitivity. These Water men have a unique ability to relate with a gentle kindness and concern that you so desperately need.

The Water Sign I prefer for you is Cancer. These men are the most emotionally responsive of the zodiac, the most ambitious, the most benevolent, and the most protective. My second choice would be Scorpio, who can be wonderful if he has a good chart. A Pisces man with a balanced chart could be great, but sometimes two Pisces people can bring out the worst in each other; you two could have a hard time making decisions and sticking to them.

Let's look at the other Emotional Element of Fire. Remember, these men possess an entirely different brand of emotion: masculine, dynamic, bold, intense, and confrontive. Which of the Fire Sign men will tend to best relate to the needs of a Water Sign lady? Depending upon many other chart factors, Sagittarius would be my first choice. Being a Mutable Sign, these men are more flexible and open-minded. You will relate to his interest in philosophy and in helping others. Leo is very family oriented, and the most devoted of the Fire Signs. But Leos really like to have things their way! The Aries man is very dynamic and exciting, and could have planet interchanges with your Sign of Pisces, being next door on the wheel. These very Martian men can really benefit from a balanced chart.

What about the Mental Sign men? They are a major mismatch! This emotional clash is the premise of this book. I know that sometimes Pisces can be very tempted by the solid Earth Sign men. Pisces women seek that stability in their lives, but think again. You will never build true emotional intimacy with a Mental Sign man. And, by the way, the Element of Earth lacks romance as part of its basic makeup.

You will also find yourself attracted to the gracious, polite, considerate nature of the Air Sign man. However, do not for a moment believe that this behavior means that he will be there for you emotionally in the way you require when the chips are down. He cannot; it is simply not part of his emotional makeup. Furthermore, a great deal of his sensitive nature pertains to his being ultratouchy about anything that he sees as criticism or an attempt to control him. And then there's his discomfort with emotion that prevents him from being emotionally supportive when you are upset. When *he* is upset, look out; you will suddenly feel emotionally abandoned as he retreats to his igloo and you receive the "arctic chill" treatment! Many Air Sign men exhibit this behavior to an extreme degree, particularly if they have too many major planets in the Air Signs. If you are still contemplating even a date with one of these men, ask yourself this: do you, or do you not, want to have a relationship that involves not only attraction and "love," but serenity and sanity as well? If you do, then listen up: these men are an absolute emotional disaster for Water women! These guys are not just on another emotional plane, they are in another emotional galaxy for you!

A Pisces lady absolutely has to have a man who provides the sense of protection that Water women need. Equally important, he must have a real understanding of your need for space and of your independent ways. He also has to be independent and self-confident in order for you to respect him. No emotional clingers for you! Though a man might get the impression from your easygoing Water demeanor that he can take control and order you around, he would make a big mistake to push a Pisces woman too far.

Let us look at one of Pisces' traits that can drive a man nuts (not to mention what it does to you). There tend to be frequent changes of mind, mood, and itinerary. While flexibility is a positive thing, if you are a Pisces who suffers from chronic changeability, it can make your life miserable. Pisces' inconsistency can make it difficult for the man in your life to feel the trust that is so important for developing true emotional intimacy. In order to feel that one can trust someone, one has to feel that one knows someone, and that naturally involves a certain amount of predictability. If you have the good fortune to have major planets in the Fixed Signs, this will be a big help in terms of follow-through!

Pisces is actually quite an emotional paradox. You are gentle and highly sensitive, with a profound need to be loved and to belong to someone. But, being an Eastern Hemisphere Sign, you have such an independent nature that you are not always able to give enough or to be there for a man if it involves canceling your plans or sacrificing your time or energy (see Chapter 8: Men Who Are Hopelessly Self-Centered). You are one very independent lady, and sometimes your natural instinct to look out for yourself could prevent you from readily doing things that are necessary to build emotional intimacy and make the other party truly feel loved.

There will never be a shortage of men who are ready and willing to meet your needs. Men are always drawn to the gentle, dreamy Pisces lady!

12

The Feeling Sign Men: Fire and Water

THE FIRE SIGN MEN: ARIES, LEO, SAGITTARIUS

Fire Type of Emotion: More passionate and intense than the other emotional element of water.

Dynamic, Confrontive, Impulsive, Enthusiastic, Perfectionistic, Futuristic, Idealistic, Romantic, Confident.

Gender: Masculine (Martian, confrontive).

Emotionally compatible only with Fire and Water women.

These men are definitely from Mars! Their masculine Fire Sun Sign makes them more Martian than men with Venusian (Water or Earth) Sun Signs. If a man has two or more additional major planets in the masculine Elements of Fire or Air, he will be a Super-Martian. It is important that a Fire chart be balanced with major planets in the feminine Elements of Water and Earth to add qualities of sensitivity, consideration, understanding, and kindness (see Chapter 5: Why Can't a Man Be More Like a Woman?).

The Fire Sign men are the most emotional, romantic, dynamic, and impulsive men of the zodiac. These men will mesmerize and inspire you with their robust enthusiasm, confidence, and courage. They are very creative and original, with great vision. Fire is the most emotionally intense and passionate Element— the Element most likely to sweep you off your feet! But, please, stop and catch your breath; it just might save you a great deal of pain and frustration. And, of course, that's what I'm here for!

Though you may be very taken with his bold, outgoing, optimistic personality, I assure you it would be too high a price to pay if you have found yourself a "spoiled child" version of the Fire Sign man. They are out there in abundance! Yes, there are some wonderful Fire Sign men, but usually only when their charts are well balanced in the other Elements.

Let's look first at some of the positive Fire qualities. Fire people define exuberance! They have a way of expressing themselves with such enthusiasm that you really feel their emotions. It was not just a great movie, it was fantastic! They do not just love someone, they worship and adore him or her! Fire is unquestionably the Element most comfortable with emotions—theirs *and* yours.

Fire is more Martian (confrontive) than the other Martian Element of Air. They do not dread the thought of confrontation, as do the Venusian (nonconfrontive) Elements of Earth and Water. Fire men are the most honest and candid of the zodiac—unfortunately, sometimes to the point of bluntness!

While emotionally mature men seem to be hard to come by in any Sign, they are going to be even harder to find in the Fire Signs. Why on earth would I think such a thing? Boyish enthusiasm, an idealistic view of life, fierce independence, a quick temper, a need for fun and recreation, excitability, rashness, impulsiveness—just the stuff maturity is made of!

And there's more great news: Fire men are the most macho-minded of the zodiac! You will regret it if you do not determine whether a Fire Sign man is adult-functioning before you become emotionally involved. If you have the misfortune to develop feelings for a Water or Earth Sign man prior to discovering that he is not an emotional grown-up, at least you will not find him to be as offensive as most Fire Sign men who have not achieved emotional maturity.

When a man has an overdose of masculine influence in his chart (too many planets in the Martian Elements of Fire or Air), he will possess a basic chauvinistic attitude toward women. Not that he exactly feels superior; he is simply of the opinion that women are just a bit inferior, in that they are not quite as capable as men. Even a man who is not a Fire Sun Sign can have so many other major planets in the Fire (and Air) Signs that he can have the same problems resulting from high Martian influence.

And you are in for another little problem with these men who have too many planets in the Martian Signs: the spoiled child mentality! They often have the emotional maturity level of a six-year-old. Any suggestion on your part that they may have done something wrong seems to give them the feeling that their mother is correcting them. Men with this imbalance are exceedingly independent, with a real need to take charge and be in control. They can be very pushy, demanding, aggressive, and even violent. They are self-centered, perfectionistic, judgmental, and dogmatic, and they think that the world revolves around them. It is not a pretty sight! Be on the lookout for a Fire Sign man to show any indication of this "I'm the Boss" routine. If he is too controlling and too impatient, or if he reacts poorly when things don't go his way on the first few dates (when he is supposedly presenting the best he has to offer), get out immediately! There is no hope for any man who shows you this side of himself when he is out to impress you. Granted, we are glad that he let the cat out of the bag so early on; now you do not have to blow your mad money on that fabulous dress for the weekend trip you will not be taking with Fire Boy!

I beg you, please do not attempt to rationalize or justify his behavior; we do not care that he has not slept for 24 hours; we all have problems. Emotional grown-ups do not take it out on others when life presents one of its many stressful scenarios; they deal with it, while managing to at least be basically civil to others.

Another problem often found with Fire men is their inability to accept their intense emotional nature. The Emotional Water men share this difficulty in coping with their feelings. Unfortunately, men have been brainwashed since childhood to regard strong emotions as something to either ignore or suppress. Harvard psychologist Ronald Levant, co-author of *Between Father and Child*, says,

> Boys are expected to detach from their mothers at an early age in order to develop their masculine identities. All too often, however, fathers are psychologically, if not physically, absent from relationships with their sons. Without being conscious of what is going on, these boys are left with a sense that autonomy is safer than intimacy. And when they grow up to become fathers and husbands, admitting feelings of attachment can be very threatening to them.

Another problem can cause Fire Sign men to be reticent about expressing their emotions. Something happens when a man has both a Fire Sun and a Fire Moon. Despite their strong Fire influence, these individuals can have difficulty getting in touch with their Fire unless they have one or more of the functional planets (Mercury, Venus, Mars) in Fire to help them express it. They tend to behave as if they lack Fire altogether. They can seem almost more like a Water Sign man. This is because, paradoxically, there is a shy side to the Element of Fire.

Incidentally, when you do find a squared-away version of a Fire Sign man, bear in mind that his independent nature will require that you give him plenty of space; no nagging!

By now you have probably gotten the idea that Fire men are too emotional to be compatible with the more emotionally reserved Earth and Air women. Regardless of the fact that any given Thinking Sign woman may have a very emotional side, she is still fundamentally not as comfortable with emotion as a Feeling Sign person. The Fire man possesses a brand of emotionality that is foreign to Earth and Air women. The Mental Sign women will feel anxious as a result of the emotional nature of a Fire man. An area of great contrast pertains to the perfectionistic Fire nature, which is always looking for a better way to do things. His ideas and suggestions are often perceived by Earth and Air Sign women as pressure or criticism.

Fire Sign men need Feeling Sign women who will understand and appreciate their emotional nature. These women will relate to the way the Fire Sign man gives emotion priority and bases decisions on what he feels. The Water Sign woman should have a major planet or two in Fire; and he needs major Water emphasis so that he can identify with her brand of ultra-sensitivity.

Eastern Hemisphere Fire Sign: Aries
Less relationship-oriented
Less concerned with the needs of others

Aries men are often the most Martian of the zodiac. Two factors would be necessary to offset this: there would need to be a strong emphasis in the Western Hemisphere, and a balance of Elements. Without at least one of these influences, he would be very self-centered.

Western Hemisphere Fire Signs: Leo, Sagittarius
More relationship-oriented
More concerned with the needs of others

While both of these Fire Sign men are going to be more needy of your attention and devotion than Aries, they are also more capable of providing you with the same. Leo will be the more devoted, and also the most in need of your devotion. Sagittarius is the most flexible and open-minded (Mutable) Sign.

The Aries Man: Fire Feeling Sign
(March 20–April 20)

ELEMENT: Fire (a bold dynamic type of emotion).

Romantic, Impulsive, Adventurous, Original, Enthusiastic, Idealistic.

EASTERN HEMISPHERE

GENDER: Masculine (Martian/confrontive).

A CARDINGAL SIGN: Energetic and ambitious.

Emotionally compatible only with Fire and Water women.

The Aries man is the most confident and adventurous Sign of the zodiac. Depending on your point of view, this man will either captivate you with his bold, dynamic personality and excite you with his vitality and sense of adventure, or overwhelm and exhaust you with his Fire intensity and Cardinal energy. And, without enough Fixed influence in his chart to follow through on the projects he is always starting, any woman could find him frustrating. Most Aries men have more than their share of problem areas. At their best (with a balanced chart and sane upbringing), they can encompass all of the wonderful Fire qualities and are capable of true compassion and an expression of romantic love that could leave you breathless!

Aries men can be exceptionally creative and original, but unfortunately one of the ways they tend to demonstrate such creativity is by constantly suggesting new and improved ways for you to do everything! They have an annoying way of always thinking that their way is *the* way! While you might initially appreciate their little pearls of originality, they have a way of wearing on one after the 400th suggestion in the span of a week and a half. Most of them truly cannot help themselves. Combine their highly inventive thinking process with their instinct for leadership: instant Mr. Let Me Show You How That Should Be Done!

With enough planets in Aries, the most Martian of the Signs, or in the other Fire and Air Signs, this man could redefine male chauvinism: the ultimate Super-Martian! Of all the masculine Signs, Aries has the greatest potential for this chauvinistic mentality.

The typical highly romantic Aries male may appear to be stuck somewhere in the fourteenth century. He can have quite a problem with the concept of women's liberation. Most women want a man who fundamentally embraces the theory of equality, even if he sometimes plays the male-female game of "Me Tarzan, you Jane." But, the typical Aries man, though he may appear to comprehend the idea of equality, doesn't actually stray far from viewing himself as a dragon slayer and a woman as his damsel in distress!

The Fire Signs are apt to have a spoiled attitude, and Aries is the most prone to this spoiled, controlling mentality. He is exceptionally headstrong. The unevolved Aries male can be hopelessly opinionated, judgmental, perfectionistic, demanding, self-centered, and dogmatic.

Impatient and headstrong, Aries has a quick temper, but he doesn't hold a grudge for long. He may explode in anger one minute, and then laugh it off the next. If his temper tantrums are unfairly directed at you, do not tolerate it for a moment. These men are easily spoiled by women who put up with their nonsense.

Incidentally, Aries men can be very jealous. Not known for doing things halfway, when an Aries man has this problem, he can be so overly protective that he may want to control your every move! (I'm sure there are some perfectly normal, functioning, considerate, thoughtful Aries men out there who can be very responsive to your needs. A cousin of a client once thought she met one in New Orleans during Mardi Gras, but admits now that it may have just been a case of too many bourbon-and-sodas!)

Which women of the zodiac will appreciate these intensely emotional men without being driven over the edge by their bold personalities and innovative suggestions? The confident Fire Sign woman will potentially be the most compatible with the Aries man. Since even an evolved Aries man is going to be a bit self-centered and pushy, a woman with the confrontive and assertive Fire nature would be able to stand her ground. A Water woman would potentially be emotionally compatible, but would need at least two major planets in the Fire Signs to hold her own with an Aries man. And he had better have major Water influence so that he can comprehend her brand of gentle sensitivity. A strong Water emphasis will help mellow out the willful and impulsive Aries traits.

Thinking Sign women (Earth and Air) will want to avoid any of the Fire Sign men, and Aries in particular! The Earth or Air lady has a more dignified, reserved, and controlled approach to emotion that does not quite mesh with this man's slightly more bombastic approach to life.

The Leo Man: Fire Feeling Sign
(July 24–August 23)

ELEMENT: Fire (a bold, dynamic type of emotion).

Enthusiastic, Idealistic, Perfectionistic, Loyal, Proud, Devoted, Creative, Romantic.

GENDER: Masculine (Martian, confrontive).

WESTERN HEMISPHERE

A FIXED SIGN: Determined and persistant.

Emotionally compatible only with Fire and Water women.

The Leo man—be prepared to worship and adore him, or forget it! That Leo the Lion, King of the Jungle thing is for real! This man has an enormous need to rule his kingdom. Any man with even one major planet in Leo will suffer from this syndrome. The man with Sun in Leo literally thrives on adoration. His Martian need for appreciation and admiration is greater than that of the other masculine Signs. He also has an enormous need to be shown the proper respect. For a Leo with other major planets also in Leo, this may stop just short of your bowing when he enters the room—actually, any Leo man could probably relate to that!

At his best, this noble and fearless cat is proud and faithful, with great generosity of spirit—happiest when basking, center stage, in the love and respect of his royal subjects! Leo may be the best of the three Fire Signs. Being a Fixed Sign, Leo has the determination and perseverance to succeed, with more sense of responsibility and follow-through than either Aries or Sagittarius.

This man is extremely efficiency-minded and takes great pride in whatever he does. He is perfectionistic; if he does something, he wants to do it well!

He is particularly concerned about and caring toward those he loves. Leo is among the three Signs that are most devoted to family and friends. If this man is truly content in his relationship with you, it is highly unlikely that he would even think of being disloyal. And your being disloyal to him is a totally foreign concept! He would be crushed beyond description! A dysfunctional Leo man who believed that his mate was unfaithful could be prone to jealous rage.

As a Fire Sign, Leo can have a real problem if there are too many additional planets in Fire. He can be anywhere from domineering and incredibly egotistical to opinionated, judgmental, and controlling. The worst manifestation of this overdose of Martian influence can make a Leo man very arrogant and even tyrannical. To make matters even more enjoyable, when a Fire Sign man has this kind of chart imbalance, he's capable of doing a remarkable impersonation of a child who has yet to figure out that the world does not revolve around his needs. He can be so wrapped up in himself that he simply loses sight of you and your needs. More than any other Sign, Leo can be obsessed with having his own way. He can also be adept at accomplishing exactly that. He even has a unique way of adopting an idea, plan, or thought of yours and making it his own!

Now, assuming that we have a Leo with a good chart, which women will show him the respect and adoration he requires without always succumbing to doing things his way? This would take either a Fire Sign woman or a Water Sign woman with enough Fire emphasis. However, Water Sign women make a note: a Fire Sign man absolutely must have major planets in your Element of Water in order to relate to your ultra-sensitive nature.

Earth and Air Sign women must avoid these Leo gentlemen; Fire Sign men are emotionally incompatible with the Mental Elements. They do not share your need to be in control of their feelings, more emotionally reserved. You will be made uncomfortable by a Leo man's brand of emotional intensity. You will think he is emotionally immature, and he will view you as being too rational and practical. With enough Venusian influence in Water or Earth, and not too much additional Fixed emphasis, a Leo man could be one of the best of the zodiac—for Fire and Water women that is!

The Sagittarius Man: Fire Feeling Sign
(November 23–December 21)

ELEMENT: Fire (a bold, dynamic type of emotion).

Enthusiastic, Idealistic, Goal-Oriented, Impulvise, Creative, Romantic, Humanitarian.

GENDER: Masculine (Martian, confrontive).

WESTERN HEMISPHERE

A MUTABLE SIGN: Flexible and changeable.

Emotionally compatible only with Fire and Water women.

The Sagittarius man is a party animal at heart—the friendly puppy dog of the zodiac—and perhaps the most freedom-oriented man of them all. Just wait until he gives you that cocker spaniel look when you ask him where he has been for the last three days! There is a wide-eyed innocence about these men. They can be so adorable! But you know what problems you can run into by spoiling cute little puppies who grow up to be unruly beasts. Read on and make sure that you are ready to cope with some of the more frustrating aspects of this fun-loving, wonderful, caring humanitarian. This man is an idealistic seeker of the truth and an avid believer in the underdog—including real dogs! Most Sagittarians have a hard time passing up a lonely stray, whether animal or human.

By the way, these guys can be incredibly touchy about rejection. Sagittarius is the most sensitive of all the Signs in this area. I know, it doesn't seem to make sense. One would think that this honor would go to one of the ultrasensitive Air or Water Signs, not to a Fire Sign. It must be that, since Sagittarians are such friendly, sincere, cheerful creatures, when that aspect of them is rejected, it is as though their very soul is being spurned! And he will probably tell you about it. The Sign of Sagittarius is the most honest of the zodiac. You will notice that I said "the Sign;" not every Sagittarius man is Honest Abe! If there are major planets next door in Scorpio (the most non-confrontive Sign of all), it can put a damper on his penchant for direct communication. If Venus is in Scorpio, he can make you crazy with his inability to tell you the truth when he fears that it will hurt your feelings.

At his best, this man could be fabulous. He personifies generosity of spirit, a passionate nature, and unbridled enthusiasm for anything that catches his fancy. If *you* catch his fancy, he might invite you to join him in his whirlwind Sagittarian exploration of the world! This man has a happy disposition and tends to view his existence as a celebration of life; there may never be a dull moment! But eventually the bills need to be paid and the lawn mowed—things that Sagittarius people view as mundane and boring. And I assure you that "boring" is not in the Fire vocabulary; they are allergic to "boring"!

These men are often little boys at heart who have somehow avoided really growing up. Somewhere deep inside, they have never lost sight of their dreams. That can be very exciting and refreshing to a fellow Fire Sign, but it might just push the typical Earth woman over the edge, as he once again seeks a new career that will be more exciting and possibly help mankind at the same time.

Which Signs are compatible with Mr. Enthusiasm? The ideal match would be a fellow Fire Sign. She will share his brand of Fire passion for life. A Water Sign woman with major planets in the Fire Signs could be compatible. There is a peculiar thing about Sagittarians: they seem instinctively resistant to the Water brand of sensitive emotional exchange. Ironically, in spite of being an Emotional Sign (Fire), Sagittarians invariably feel almost embarrassed to verbalize their feelings for you in too sentimental a manner.

Sagittarians dislike any kind of weakness, and they tend to view too much tender emotion as a of display of weakness. They do not do well with being sick or hospitalized. Nothing about their independent, indestructible, fiery nature can relate to being physically limited in any way.

The more emotionally reserved Thinking Sign women of Earth and Air are not compatible with this gentleman, who exudes emotional vigor. These women will perceive a Fire man to be too emotionally needy, which makes Thinking Sign women feel pressured and anxious. His more robust, bold approach to love does not blend well with their more cautious, controlled emotional nature.

Incidentally, Sagittarian men are often perceived as having a know-it-all attitude, and can have a spoiled-child mentality. Sagittarius also has a rather innocent way of automatically assuming that others feel what they feel, like what they like, and simply have to believe what they believe. They are often sincerely astonished by the fact that this may not be the case. They can also have a problem handling frustration, and they abhor stupidity.

Being a Fire Sign, Sagittarius lives in the future with all its endless possibilities. If you need a man to whom responsibility, with all of its confining rules, is highly valued, this is not the man! He will probably do his best in this department as long as it doesn't interfere too much with his recreational and social calendar.

Sagittarians are very slow to mature. They also can be hard to catch. If you have your sights set on one, give him all the space he needs or forget it! I am telling you that the issues of freedom and independence are almost a religion to this Sign!

THE WATER SIGN MEN: CANCER, SCORPIO, PISCES

WATER BRAND OF EMOTION: More gentle and sensitive than the other Feeling Element of Fire.

Kind, Sympathetic, Compassionate, Understanding, Forgiving, Thoughtful, Giving, Helpful, Considerate.

GENDER: Feminine (Venusian, nonconfrontive).

Emotionally compatible only with Water and Fire women.

These men are from Venus, at least in terms of their feminine Water Sun Sign. The more additional major planets they have in the feminine (Venusian) Elements of Water and Earth, the more they will be on a woman's wavelength. However, there can be a problem with Water Sign men being too Venusian (too nonconfrontive, too giving to others, and so on) if there are not enough major planets in the Martian Elements of Air and Fire (see Chapter 5: Why Can't a Man Be More Like a Woman?).

The Water Sign men are the most emotionally sensitive of the zodiac. If you are a Feeling Sign woman (Water or Fire), you will relish the fact that, unlike the Air or Earth Sign men who "think" their emotions, these Water Sign men will *feel* their emotions. This will help you to experience your feelings on an emotional, rather than a mental, level. These men, who are so gracious, nurturing, sympathetic, forgiving, and ultra-sensitive, truly need someone who understands their intensely emotional nature. They need a woman who can relate to them with the same gentle qualities, thereby making them feel loved.

Though I recommend Water Sign men as potentially compatible for both Fire and Water women, the Water woman is the better match in that she operates on the same extremely sensitive Water wavelength. For a Fire Sign woman, a Water Sign man would need a strong Fire emphasis so that he could relate to her impulsive, fiery nature, and ideally she should have a solid Water influence in her chart in order to understand his extreme sensitivity.

The typical Earth or Air woman would ultimately be uncomfortable with this man's highly emotional nature, and would not be able to relate to his level of need for emotional support.

Now let us take a look at some of the problem areas you will encounter with these supersensitive men. A Water Sign man with more than a total of three major planets in the Water Signs could be so overly touchy that he would imagine insults or offenses where they do not exist. He will be made anxious by even constructive comments, which he perceives as a criticism of him. A man with a high Water influence may not have the perspective to separate his immediate emotional interpretation from what is actually transpiring. Once he jumps to feeling criticized, he will most likely have lost all objectivity. He will not be able to see that you are not upset with him, but with the situation—or that perhaps you have a good reason to be upset with him (a Water Sign man does not deal well with the concept of someone being upset with him). It can be hard for him to hear the other person's point of view without feeling that it is a personal attack. Mercury in an Earth Sign, which would add logic and perspective, can help to offset this problem.

If he has four or more major planets in the Water Signs, somewhere along the way he would have required some "swimming lessons" to help him cope with all that emotion. You might want to do yourself a favor: throw him a life jacket, wish him luck, and head for shore! Men often have trouble handling this depth of Water feeling, this feminine brand of emotion. The world demands of men that they be strong, stable, and emotionally tough! This can make life very difficult, not just for men with a Water Sun Sign, but for any man with more than two major planets in the Feeling Elements of Water or Fire.

Harvard psychologist Ronald Levant, co-author of *Between Father and Child,* says:

> In general, women have a much easier time verbalizing their feelings than men. When men are disappointed, hurt or afraid, they may be unable to put their feelings into words. Instead, they are

likely to experience a tightness in the throat, a pain in the stomach, an elevated heart rate, or even just a sense of antsiness.

Men are finally beginning to understand that feelings are not feminine—that feelings are human!

I tend to recommend Cancer over the other two Water Signs. Cancer men are unquestionably the most devoted, the most relationship-oriented, and the most emotionally responsive, and they tend to be adept at money management. While all the Water Signs can be too nonconfrontive, Scorpio men often have a major problem in this area. Pisces men are a bit secretive, and are often either confused or indecisive about their emotions. However, any of the Water Signs can be wonderful for Feeling Sign Women if their overall chart is balanced.

Eastern Hemisphere Water Sign: Pisces
Less relationship-oriented
Less concerned with the needs of others

Because the Eastern Hemisphere Signs are generally more concerned with themselves, and less concerned with your needs, a Pisces man may not be as responsive to you as you would like him to be.

Western Hemisphere Water Signs: Cancer, Scorpio
More relationship-oriented
More concerned with the needs of others

Being in the Western Hemisphere makes Cancer and Scorpio more likely to care about your needs and respond to them. Cancer is the most benevolent and emotionally responsive of all the Signs.

The Cancer Man: Water Feeling Sign
(June 22–July 23)

ELEMENT: Water (a loving, gentle nurturing type of emotion).

Loving, Benevolent, Ambitious, Sentimental, Sympathetic, Considerate, Kind, Gentle, Sincere.

GENDER: Feminine (Venusian, nonconfrontive).

WESTERN HEMISPHERE SIGN

A CARDINAL SIGN: Energetic and Ambitious.

Emotionally compatible only with Water and Fire women.

The Cancer man is the most benevolent and emotionally responsive of all the Signs. If you find a good one, I simply cannot recommend this man highly enough. He is my favorite of the Water Signs, more in touch with his feelings and more confrontive than Scorpio, and more action-oriented and decisive than Pisces. Being a Western Hemisphere Sign and, therefore, more inclined toward relationships, he is the most needy one of the bunch; he may or may not own up to this. This man needs to be needed; he yearns to be adored and fussed over. He must feel your love. But, in return, you will feel his; he is the most emotionally responsive, the most emotionally connective of the Signs.

Cancer and Capricorn are the two most moody Signs of the zodiac. However, when the Cancer man is in the mood to make you feel loved, no one does it better! The cause of these changing emotions is that Cancer is ruled by the ever-changing Moon. This seems to give the Cancer man a very appealing, almost shy or elusive quality. And, it would stand to reason that, with his ultrasensitivity and poetic nature, he would be very nostalgic—a true sentimentalist!

He is also very much the homebody and extremely family-oriented, especially if he has planets in Leo or Virgo. Cancer people are so devoted to close friends and family that, if they really care for you or are touched by your plight, there is very little they would not do for you.

If emotionally mature, this man makes a wonderful father. Being so genuinely interested in and responsive to the feelings and ideas of others, he is unusually concerned and caring about the little one's needs. Speaking of children, when he feels hurt or criticized, Cancer the Crab will withdraw into his shell, like a child hiding in his room, until a warm, friendly face coaxes him out. And if it is your friendly face, he will kiss it and forgive you because that is his nature. But if this happens too many times, you may have to leave him alone for quite a while before you attempt to lure him out again. Leaving him alone may sometimes be a good idea anyway; Cancers love a challenge! There can be a fine line between making him feel loved and needed, and smothering him. Play a little hard to get. Be patient; he could be worth it. He will take care of you financially (Cancers are good with money), emotionally (your cup will overflow), and physically (Cancer men are extremely protective of women and children). But ironically, though they are innately very protective, Cancer men tend to be made uncomfortable by women who specifically seek their support and are, therefore, attracted to strong women.

Does all this sound too good to be true? Are there any problem areas? Of course there are. We have already seen that he can be a bit moody and may retreat to sulk. This makes Cancer men emotionally unpredictable, and some of them have a real problem with moodiness. At his worst, this man can be very sullen and pessimistic. Cancers can be ridiculously touchy when it comes to feeling that you are being critical of them, particularly if they have planets in Virgo. Some Cancer men, especially if women have spoiled them rotten, have some emotional growing up to do even though they may be well past forty. Cancer men can be the babies of the zodiac when they have not matured emotionally.

With whom are these profoundly emotional men compatible? Water Sign women are definitely the best match, in that they will be on the same ultrasensitive wavelength. Fire women with a strong Water influence are also potentially compatible. But the Cancer man in question would need to have a solid Fire emphasis in his chart; otherwise, he would lack the fiery qualities and the bold, dynamic approach to love that she requires. A Leo lady could be a good match for Cancer, since she might have planets next door in Cancer. My second choice would be Sagittarius. An Aries lady might be too emotionally independent for a needy Cancer man.

Earth and Air women operate on too much of a mental plane for these men. The Cancer man's deep, brooding, ultra-sensitive brand of emotionality is something to which they will have a hard time relating. Cancer needs to be related to in a very emotional way that is foreign to Earth and Air women. These Thinking Sign women need to be in the mood to express their feelings; the Cancer man needs to feel that you are always there for him emotionally! You will think he is too needy and insecure. He will perceive you as being emotionally removed and analytical.

The Scorpio Man: Water Feeling Sign
(October 24–November 22)

ELEMENT: Water (a loving, gentle nurturing type of emotion).

Highly Emotionally Charged, Courageous, Forceful, Persistent, Secretive, Suspicious, Intuitive.

GENDER: Feminine (Venusian, nonconfrontive).

WESTERN HEMISPHERE

A FIXED SIGN: Determined and persistent.

Emotionally compatible only with Water and Fire women.

Though the Scorpio man is charged with an emotional intensity unequaled by any other Sign, the typical Scorpio man will strive to present himself to the world as calm, cool, and collected at all times. Scorpios possess a great deal of self-control. Combined with willpower, tenacity, perseverance, determination, and an aura of supreme self-confidence, this creates a magnetism that many women find irresistible. And Scorpio knows this! Hence, the many Scorpio men who manage to somehow work their Sun Sign into their opening monologue. You are now supposed to be under their magic spell!

Scorpio is also the most mysterious Sign of the zodiac. These men can be very private, secretive, and nonconfrontive (more about that in a minute). You may know a Scorpio for years, and yet find yourself wondering whether you know him at all. One of the reasons he is so nonconfrontive is that he simply may not have confronted himself in terms of what he is feeling or thinking—in which case he cannot very well share it with you! An incredibly useful psychological tool called "active listening" (described in the book *I'm Okay, You're Okay,* by Dr. Thomas A. Harris) comes in handy with a Scorpio, to help dredge up those hidden feelings that are often buried deep within.

An emotionally or mentally disturbed Scorpio who is operating from this Sign's most negative energies could be a very scary proposition. A really dysfunctional Scorpio man can have a cruel, almost evil quality. Due to the very subconscious side of this Sign, he can have a major problem with passive-aggressive behavior. He may have to win at all cost. If he thinks that you have "caused" him to feel upset or angry, or if you "make him lose" in any way, watch out! He will get back at you somehow. He may not appear to be the least bit upset, due to his strong need to be in control, as well as not wishing to give you the satisfaction of thinking you have hurt him in any way.

Scorpio can have a vague or distracted quality that can be very frustrating. It is as though he is not hearing what you are saying; perhaps he is so lost in his private world that he has to stop to tune back in to this world. With three or more major planets in Scorpio—particularly when this involves Mercury—you may have a man who literally does not hear what you are saying to him when you do not have his undivided, eye-contact attention.

With whom are these emotionally charged men compatible? Certainly not Thinking Sign women, who are not particularly comfortable with emotion for starters. However, Earth and Air women can sometimes be fooled into thinking that these men are on their more mental wavelength. This is because of that Scorpio penchant for control at all cost, resulting from the fear of their deeply emotional side. They tend to function through their planets in the Thinking Signs, and they do quite a good impersonation of an Earth or Air Sign man.

But, being the highly emotional creatures that they are, whether or not they are willing to show it, they will usually feel crushed and unfulfilled in a relationship with a Thinking Sign woman. She simply will not be on a Scorpio man's emotional wavelength, and will have great difficulty picking up on his needs, which he may or may not verbalize. Then, when these unexpressed needs are not met, he will be upset with her, and no doubt proceed to exhibit that lovely passive-aggressive behavior. Then, when asked, "What's the matter?" he will reply, "Matter? Nothing is the matter! Why on earth would you think anything is the matter?" Now is about the time many of us would be contemplating whether we will let him keep the Miles Davis CD collection when the household items are divided up. The ultimate in crazy-making behavior is possible from a Scorpio who is not an emotional grown-up!

It really takes a fellow Water Sign woman (or perhaps a Fire Sign woman with major planets in the Water Signs) to fully understand this man's brand of ultraemotionality. A Fire Sign woman with major planets in the Water Signs would be potentially compatible with a Scorpio who had enough Fire influence in order to relate to her fiery qualities.

The woman in this Scorpio man's life had also better be prepared to give him a great deal of freedom. Ironically, when he has it, he probably won't make much use of it because he is extremely relationship-oriented. Scorpio is much more in need of feeling free to do as he pleases than one might think. They do not deal well with the stress of feeling obligated to respond in a particular way unless they have made the decision to do so (again, this really applies to *all* men to a greater or lesser extent). Of course, with a Scorpio man, you may not know what's going on due to their infamous "all is well with the world" exterior. He may simply announce one day that he is leaving—after he has found another safe harbor that is! Scorpio men do not like being without a relationship.

When you find a Scorpio who has all of his emotional ducks in a row (which may take some luck), he will demonstrate all of those wonderful Water traits: he will be gentle, considerate, gracious, kind, and loving. This very thoughtful man will genuinely care about your needs, perhaps even too much so. He will love you with all the passion of this intensely emotional Sign.

The Pisces Man: Water Feeling Sign (February 19–March 20)

ELEMENT: Water (a loving, gentle nurturing type of emotion).

Loving, Understanding, Sympathetic, Forgiving, Compassionate, Intuitive, Perceptive, Changeable.

GENDER: Feminine (Venusian, nonconfrontive).

EASTERN HEMISPHERE

A MUTABLE SIGN: Flexible and changeable.

Emotionally compatible only with Water and Fire women.

The Pisces man is a compassionate, caring man with a cheerful, gentle, poetic nature and an almost dreamlike quality. He cannot tolerate seeing another living creature in pain. Unfortunately, this dreamy quality can cause problems. Pisces is ruled by Neptune, the planet of illusion, delusion, and confusion. Some of these men can have difficulty detecting the difference between their illusions and reality; the more additional planets they have in Pisces, the more difficult this could be. Pisces men can become possessed by their imagination and the need to escape into their own world—a world without pain and harsh realities. You could be spending a good deal of time just trying to figure out which world he is operating from at any given moment.

He is so aware of the nuances of human relationships that his feelings can be hurt by a simple slight which someone else might not even notice. This ultrasensitivity means that his mate will need to be very sensitive as well, and very tuned in to his needs. This man yearns to be understood emotionally; he needs endless emotional support and encouragement. Pisceans are usually quite cheerful and gregarious. Being of a Mutable Sign, they are also flexible and changeable, although there is a fine line between being flexible and being indecisive. Sometimes a Pisces man's inability to make a decision that he sticks to could make you want to tear your hair out.

This man will frequently feel confused about his emotions, including his feelings about you. You may have to be prepared to hang in there long enough for him to sort it out if you are truly interested in him. But, do not pressure him, whatever you do! This Water Sign man may have even less ability to handle stress and pressure than either Cancer or Scorpio. His unique brand of non-confrontiveness may include saying anything to pacify you at the moment. Pisces has a pronounced tendency to lie or distort the truth. This can become such a habit that a Pisces man will lie when there is no reason not to simply tell you the truth in the first place. If you need full disclosure, Pisces just may not be the Sign for you.

Another thing to bear in mind regarding Pisces men is that they are prone to give up too readily—on relationships, dreams, goals, jobs, hobbies, or you—when things are not going well, when they feel the situation is hopeless, or when they feel defeated. This inability to hang in there when the going gets rough, can be a real problem for many of these men. They are just so incredibly sensitive and, unfortunately, this cold cruel world we live in tends to require a certain hard-core reality factor in order to survive. Reality is not usually a Pisces strong point. Major planets in Earth will make this highly sensitive man more confident and grounded.

Pisces men are sometimes emotionally undependable; feelings and thoughts that they sincerely express to you could change in a heartbeat. Water does not have form or shape; it tends to flow all over the place. After all, Pisces is Mutable (flexible) Water!

By the way, do not expect that, just because he needs lots of love, attention, and support, the Pisces man will always be there for you. Pisces is Eastern Hemisphere (self-oriented), and unless there is a major influence in the Western Hemisphere in his chart, the more self-directed aspects of this Eastern emphasis will prevail.

Pisces men are recommended for Water Sign women, and for Fire Sign women with enough Water in their charts. Only women with major Water emphasis will understand this Water brand of extreme sensitivity, and be able to cope with his frequent mood changes.

When it comes to Pisces men and Fire women, there could be some problem areas even though both are Emotional Elements. He needs major planets in Fire in order to match her brand of intense Fire emotion. Fire is bold and confident, spontaneous and impulsive! The reverse is true as well: a Fire woman without enough Water could lack the gentle, mellow Water qualities so important to the Pisces man. Also, the Fire woman's penchant for honesty would be sorely compromised by the Piscean version of the truth.

The Thinking women (Earth and Air) are definitely not on this man's emotional plane. At any given moment, his plane could take off to a dream world that would be foreign to them indeed. The analytical Air woman (despite the romance in her soul) and the practical Earth lady would get lost on this flight. He would be wondering why she cannot relate to his dreams; she would be asking herself why this man cannot think a little more rationally and keep both feet on the ground.

Earth and Air People:
Thinking Has Priority

13

The Thinking Sign Women:
Earth and Air

THE EARTH SIGN WOMEN: TAURUS, VIRGO, CAPRICORN

EARTH TYPE OF THINKING: Practical, Down-to-Earth, Literal, Detail-Minded, Conventional, Cautious, Realistic.

GENDER: Feminine (Venusian, nonconfrontive).

Emotionally compatible only with Earth and Air men.

If you are an Earth Sign woman, you will probably have a very earthy approach to life and to love. Even given your frivolous or impulsive moments and fantasies, you basically have a more practical and conventional attitude toward romance.

Earth Sign women have a natural discomfort with processing too much emotion. The Thinking Signs of Earth and Air are fundamentally somewhat uncomfortable with the emotional side of life. You are more at home with thoughts and facts than with feelings.

You need a man whose approach to emotionality is similar—a man who, like you, will not relate to too much overt emotional display. You also need a man of substance who is realistic, trust-worthy, and dependable. Earth Sign men (Taurus, Virgo, Capri-corn) are potentially the most compatible. These men will not be inclined to pressure you emotionally or need you to always show them how you feel. You will appreciate Earth Sign men for everything from their basic common sense to their logical rea-soning process. In order for you to feel secure and safe, you ab-solutely cannot have any doubts as to whether the bills are going to be paid. None of the ultrasensitive, artistic Water or impulsive, extravagant Fire types for you!

To illustrate the extreme gap in emotional wavelengths that can exist between you Earth ladies and those intensely roman-tic Fire gentlemen, let me share with you the following enlight-ening episode; it proved to my Leo friend that he and his lady love were perhaps not a perfect match.

Hollywood, California, circa late 1980s, opening of the Hol-lywood Bowl: my Leo (Fire, Feeling) friend, in a sincere effort to show his undying love and devotion to his Virgo (Earth, Thinking) wife on their tenth anniversary, came up with the following elaborate, costly extravaganza as a means of cele-brating this momentous event. He arranged for a horse-drawn carriage (six white horses, no less) to magically carry them to opening night at the Bowl! What woman would not die for a man who would even *think* of such a thing? Apparently an Earth lady with no real fire emphasis in her chart. She was ap-palled! How could this man spend hard-earned money that they could ill afford on such nonsense? Needless to say, she put an immediate halt to the project. What pushed her over the brink was that he had contacted the media; she (with her shy Cancer moon) was not about to be embarrassed by having the world see that she was married to such a lunatic (that is the Earth interpretation of one capable of such folly)! This poor man had gone through such effort—he had to apply for a parade permit, made nonrefundable deposits, and even paid extra to have the white horses bathed so that they would be sparkling white for the TV cameras!

As it turned out, he is now married to a woman on his Fire wavelength, and they probably spend all their money on romantic weekends. I hope that his Virgo former wife found a man whose romantic urges are confined to more rational and affordable adventures.

Now let's take a serious look at the extreme emotional incompatibility of Earth women and Fire Sign men (Aries, Leo, Sagittarius). Earth is fundamentally more dignified and reserved in its approach to emotional matters; Fire is the most comfortable with Feeling. His mere emotional intensity can make Earth women uncomfortable. You have a fundamental fear of too much exchange of emotion, and you like to be in control of your feelings!

This gap is enormous between the Earth and Fire Signs in the way they relate to emotionality. But there is also a great difference in their innate approach to life in general. One is practical, responsible, and cautious and lives in the here and now; the other is emotional, irreverent, and impulsive, and lives for the future.

Furthermore, Fire Sign men can have problems that would really push an Earth Sign woman over the brink. When they have too many planets in the masculine Elements of Fire or Air, they are unlikely to be emotionally mature. This results in what I call overly masculine behavior (see Chapter 6: The Male Chauvinist, Astrologically Defined). This includes an extreme level of independence, impatience, dominance, and judgmental nature—and, in some cases, a potential for violence. He has a real urge to control others. As upsetting as this can be for another Fire Sign, it would be even more mind-boggling and anxiety-producing for an Earth or Air Sign woman.

Water Sign men are also a Thinker-Feeler clash with Earth women. A Cancer, Scorpio, or Pisces man possesses a deeply brooding type of emotion. In this match, the two of you would approach life in totally different ways. He is ultrasensitive and makes important decisions based on how he feels. You, on the other hand, make decisions as a result of looking at the facts.

He would tend to see an Earth Sign woman as emotionally re-moved and too practical. You would view him as someone who needs to grow up emotionally.

What about the Air Sign men (Gemini, Libra, Aquarius)? Like your Element of Earth, Air is a mental Element, and there-fore also emotionally independent and in control of feelings. Bear in mind, though, that Air is a different type of thinking. While Earth is reasonable, logical, and practical, Air is abstract, analytical, and idealistic. These men can be like a breath of fresh air to a more pragmatic Earth woman.

A final note: you need to be aware of a problem that causes many Earth Sign individuals a great deal of difficulty in rela-tionships. As a Venusian Element, Earth is fundamentally non-confrontive, which makes it uncomfortable for you to be candid and direct concerning your feelings and your needs. This is not just in terms of expressing your needs to others, but even when it comes to knowing or understanding them your-self. While there are certainly some Earth women who have enough Air and Fire in their charts to make them more at ease with confrontation, they will still not like heavily emotional conversations or dealing with people who are in a highly emo-tional state. It's important for Earth Sign people to realize that you can let others know how you feel without having the con-versation escalate to this level. Read Chapter 10: Why Some Men Find It Difficult to Tell You How They Feel, to better un-derstand how crucial it is to your emotional health, and that of your relationships, to consistently share your feelings with your mate.

The Taurus Woman: Earth Thinking Sign
(April 21–May 21)

ELEMENT: Earth (a logical, practical type of thinking).

Reliable, Patient, Possessing Great Fortitude, Stubborn, Sensuous.

GENDER: Feminine (Venusian, nonconfrontive).

A FIXED SIGN: Determined and persistent.

Emotionally compatible only with Earth and Air Sign men.

Is Taurus stubborn? As one Taurus client of mine put it, "I simply have an unwavering mindset!"—a fact of which she was quite proud! It would not hurt Taurus to be just a bit more open to the possibility of changing your mind, even after you have made what you thought was your final decision. Wouldn't it be dreadful to miss out on what might have been the relationship of a lifetime due to a lack of open-mindedness?

Taurus is ruled by Venus, the planet of love and beauty. Is it any wonder that Taureans love that which is both useful and beautiful? This Sign also has a powerful love for the beauty and grandeur of this earth. Of all the Signs, none would love more the role of Mistress of the Country Manor—to have a magnificent home filled with beautiful things (oak-paneled rooms, stained-glass windows, velvet drapes), set in the countryside they so love.

Which men of the zodiac will be most compatible with Taurus? One is often very good with one's own Sign, but bear in mind that with your Sign being Fixed (persistent and determined), there could be a problem if both of you are too "Fixed" in your thinking. Both of you would need major planets in the Mutable Signs to add flexibility. If he has a good chart, and is emotionally mature, a Taurus man could make a wonderful mate; they are devoted and loyal companions.

Capricorn could also make an excellent mate for Ms. Taurus. These men are among the brightest and the funniest of the zodiac. However, depending upon their charts, they can be manipulative and overly serious (oddly enough, still possessing that wonderful Capricorn wry sense of humor). The Earth Sign of Virgo is gentle, sensitive, and caring—and very devoted!

What about the other Mental Elements of Air (Gemini, Libra, Aquarius)? Earth Sign women will relate to these intelligent,

communicative men with whom they can potentially be emotionally compatible. However, Air is a different type of Thinking: abstract and analytical. An Air Sign man would ideally have
major planets in the Earth Signs to bring him down to earth.

Assuming we have an Air Sign man whose chart is reason-
ably well balanced, my first choice among them for Taurus
would be Libra. This Sign is also ruled by the planet Venus,
and Libra men will share your profound love of the beautiful
things in this universe. Gemini would be my second choice of
the Air Sign men. But Gemini men can be very changeable and
may be too unpredictable. However, if you have planets next
door in Gemini, it would give you something in common with
this restless, multifaceted man—and, of course, he could have
planets in Taurus, which would help with compatibility. The
Aquarius man would usually be the least desirable of the Air
Sign men. When they have too many planets in the Martian
Signs, they can have a serious problem with "overly masculine"
behavior. However, an Aquarius man with a balanced chart
could make an excellent mate for a Taurus woman.

As a Taurus, with a penchant for possessions, you can also
be rather possessive when it comes to the man in your life. You
should, therefore, avoid men with too independent a nature
who would feel smothered or controlled by any indication of
this—a good reason to avoid the freedom-oriented Fire Sign
men (who all clash with Earth anyway!) and any Air Sign men
who lack a balanced chart. Of the masculine Signs, the Air Sign
of Libra is something of an exception due to its being the least
prone to "overly masculine" behavior.

Fire Sign men and Water Sign men are out of the question; all
six of these Signs are on a totally different emotional wavelength
(see Chapter 3: The Clash Between Feelers and Thinkers). Taurus is an Earth Sign, and is more reserved and less comfortable
with emotion. The Feeling Elements of Fire and Water have a
very emotional nature (whether they initially appear that way
or not), and have a manner of expressing these feelings that

makes Earth Sign women uncomfortable. The Martian Element of Fire is a brand of intense, passionate emotion that can make you think he is possessive or controlling. And the ultrasensitive Water Sign man requires a woman who will be sensitive and responsive to his emotional needs, particularly if he has other major planets in the Water Signs. He has a strong need to feel emotionally connected to a woman in a way that would only tend to make you feel pressured or restrained.

Incidentally, Taureans have to watch out for two problem areas that can cause difficulties within a relationship. The Element of Earth is feminine (Venusian) and fundamentally nonconfrontive. Therefore, you will sometimes tolerate a negative attitude or poor treatment from others rather than confront them. However, if you have major planets in Fire or Air, it will make you more comfortable with speaking your mind. It is extremely important, in terms of building emotional intimacy, to let people know how you feel and what you need!

The second area of difficulty relates to Taurus being in the Eastern Hemisphere (see Chapter 8: Men Who Are Hopelessly Self-Centered). While the positive aspects of Eastern Hemisphere influence (self-confidence and independence) are wonderful, the negative side, which causes one to be too emotionally independent, can spell relationship trouble. Your mate needs to feel that you will go out of your way for him when he really needs you. Many Eastern Hemisphere people are not always able to make their mates feel loved enough.

Now let's look at something positive about the Fixed Sign of Taurus. When a person's chart has more than two major planets in any of the four Fixed Signs (Taurus, Leo, Scorpio, Aquarius), that person will have a great deal of perseverance and determination—a real capacity to follow through with projects, to see things through to their conclusion. The strongest Fixed quality is found in the Sign of Taurus the Bull! This is due to the combination of the Fixed Mode and the Earth Element, creating the greatest level of determination. However, we don't want you to apply your tremendous stamina, fortitude, and ability to withstand physical and emotional discomfort to enduring a disastrous astrological match! Please hold out for the dependable, responsible, trustworthy, romantic soul you need and deserve. Believe me, you will always have your share of men who will be taken by your terrific Taurus traits; you are a warm, friendly, funny, patient, thoughtful, generous, sensuous, loyal, and devoted companion!

The Virgo Woman: Earth Thinking Sign
(August 24–September 23)

ELEMENT: Earth (a logical, practical brand of thinking).

Conscientious, Discriminating, Methodical, Thoughtful, Helpful, Kind, Devoted.

GENDER: Feminine (Venusian, nonconfrontive).

WESTERN HEMISPHERE

A MUTABLE SIGN: Flexible and changeable.

Emotionally compatible only with Earth and Air men.

Virgo is Ms. Discriminating! Shady, questionable types need not apply. While your Earth sisters may occasionally go for the mountain man type, this man would not be your cup of tea. Virgo may be an Earth Sign, but the Virgo woman is not as earthbound as the Taurus or Capricorn female. There is just something about your sweet, gentle nature that tends to offset the more typical earthiness. The highly discerning Virgo woman possesses a certain refinement that even a dignified Capricorn lady may not quite capture! And with Virgo being in the Western Hemisphere (more relationship-oriented), you are more needy of others and more considerate of their feelings.

But you are indeed an Earthy lady who is logical, practical, reliable, determined, and trustworthy. Virgo is among the three Signs (Cancer, Leo, Virgo) that are the most devoted to loved ones. You are extremely giving and loving to those you care about, and you need a man who is also very caring and protective toward you.

The man in your life must also have a strong Earth influence. No overly idealistic, fantasy-oriented gentlemen for you; they might forget to pay the rent, or worse yet, not have the money to pay it! Virgo, more than any other Sign, must have a sense of security. You can't relate to a lifestyle without order and predictability. You may indeed enjoy moments of spontaneity (particularly if you have planets in the Fire Signs), but when it comes to the functional aspects of life, you have a practical, methodical approach. Not every Virgo needs to have organized closets and cupboards (that depends on how many planets they have in Virgo), but there is always a need for order when it comes to life in general: where you live, where you work, and so on. Virgos hate it when these life issues are unresolved. They are not going to feel comfortable or safe in any kind of un-settled environment. (Your Virgo cat will not appreciate your relocating his bed or cat chow bowl.) Virgos are not inclined to accept a job that involves commission sales or irregular paychecks.

In this respect, Earth men are ideal for Virgo women. These men will not only share your need for logic and reason, but you will relate to their earthy approach to love and romance. While one's own Sign is sometimes a good match (you will appreciate each other's affectionate ways and devoted nature), two Virgos together could spend too much time worrying about everything. Both Capricorn and Taurus could bring more confidence and stability to the relationship. Capricorn also has a sense of family tradition and a need for accomplishment, and will share your penchant for details. However, Capricorn men can be manipulative and overly serious, in spite of their wry wit. Taurus possesses a great sense of humor, and is a loyal and devoted companion.

What about the Element of Air? Although Virgo is compatible with Air since they are both Thinking Signs, when Air Sign men have too much Air influence, they can turn their normally gentle air breeze into an arctic chill. You would need an Air man without too many planets in Air, and preferably a planet or two in your Element of Earth.

When Air Sign men have an overall balanced chart, they can be quite compatible with Virgo women. Libra would be my first recommendation of the Air Sign men. With Libra being the Sign next to Virgo, you might have some planet interchanges. The other two Air Signs of Aquarius and Gemini, being in the Eastern Hemisphere, are less relationship-minded and less concerned with your needs. Aquarius is a Fixed Sign, making these men very attached to their own point of view. Aquarius men can be very controlling and self-centered. And Gemini men are often not the best match for you, even though both of your Signs are ruled by Mercury. Their restless nature and unpredictability can leave you feeling anxiety-ridden.

Now let's look at the Signs to be avoided at all cost. Fire Sign men are an astrological disaster for Virgo women. This mismatch is a classic example of the Thinker-Feeler clash. Your Sign of Virgo, with its more reserved and contained approach to the expression of feelings, is a particular clash with these intensely emotional men. And when a Fire Sign man has too many major planets in the Fire Signs, he can do an outstanding impersonation of a spoiled child. This may stop just short of holding his breath until he gets his way. He's likely to exhibit everything from an impatient, demanding attitude to very controlling behavior.

What about the other Emotional Element of Water? Like Fire, Water clashes with your Mental Element, and is not emotionally compatible with the practical Earth ladies. Read Chapter 12: The Feeling Sign Men: Fire and Water, to fully understand how Water and Fire men are on an entirely different emotional wavelength. What is confusing is that Water Sign men have a very gentle, tender side to which a sensitive Virgo lady may be very attracted. You will definitely have a certain sensitivity in common, but the difference between a Mental and an Emotional Sign comes into play in the way they express all these sensitive thoughts and feelings. The Water Sign men have a deep, brooding brand of emotionality that makes Earth women uncomfortable. You want a man who will appreciate you, not label you as too practical and unemotional.

Incidentally, there is a problem which virtually all Virgos need to work on. Virgo is one of the most nonconfrontive Signs; you are fundamentally uncomfortable with bringing up any subject that might escalate into an argument or dispute. Earth people instinctively suppress their needs and feelings, frequently not even knowing what those feelings are, much less being able to share them with others. You must learn to let others know how you feel (see Chapter 5: Why Can't a Man be More Like a Woman? to learn more about the problems experienced by all of the Venusian Signs in terms of their instinctive inability to express their feelings and be confrontive). The essence of building emotional intimacy is sharing both your likes and your dislikes with the other party. This is also a key ingredient in reducing stress—something of great importance to Virgo, one of the Signs most prone to having problems with stress.

Virgos are very sensitive to criticism. Sometimes Virgos seem to almost manufacture criticism where it doesn't exist. Please attempt to be objective about what you are hearing, and realize that the other party may just be making a helpful suggestion that was in no way meant as critical.

And finally, because Virgos are exceptionally devoted to family and intimates, and need to be helpful to others, they must watch out for the strong tendency to go overboard in these areas. It is very common for Virgos, especially Virgo women, to give so much to others that they do not allow enough time and energy for their own needs.

The Capricorn Woman: Earth Thinking Sign
(December 22–January 20)

ELEMENT: Earth (a logical, practical brand of thinking).

Accomplishment-Oriented, Literal, Traditional,
Discriminating, Realistic.

GENDER: Feminine (Venusian, nonconfrontive).

EASTERN HEMISPHERE

A CARDINAL SIGN: Energetic and ambitious.

Emotionally compatible only with Earth and Air men.

Capricorn, if you were to put your mind to it, you could win
a dating marathon hands down! Ms. Goat, in top form, will
continue up the mountain path as all competitors fall by the
wayside! If you have been single for a long time, take heart. Assuming that this is a situation you are looking to remedy (many
Capricorn women seem quite content with the single life),
yours is the Sign to make it happen. The extremely powerful
and winning combination of Earth determination and Cardinal
ambition and stamina is something to behold! If you set your
sights on something, or someone, all others need not apply.

You are the most competitive and serious Sign in the zodiac.
To say that many Capricorns are inclined toward overserious-
ness is like saying that Rush Limbaugh is slightly right-wing.
But, in all fairness, one can readily sympathize with Capricorn's
tendency toward being a Serious Sally. Ruled by the very stern
Saturn (the planet of discipline, restriction, caution, and restraint), Capricorn's sense of duty, responsibility, and propriety
is enormous. If there were an additional major planet or two in
Capricorn, you could have the problem of not only having to
do everything, but having to do it all properly! This could put a
great deal of pressure on you. You must make every effort to
lighten up; stress reduction classes are in order here!

Thank goodness for the Capricorn sense of humor—or I should say sense of the absurd and ridiculous? I am convinced that all of the truly irreverent comedy writers must have major Capricorn influence in their charts. There is just something about this Sign that finds humor in the bitter ironies of this insane world. One of the most humorous aspects of human behavior has to be the embarrassing truths we attempt to hide behind transparent masks—especially transparent to Capricorns who can see right through the facades! And I might add that not only do you perceive the world more accurately than any other Sign, but you are also the most logical, practical, and literal-minded Sign of the zodiac. You have great respect for that which is useful, and little patience for anything that is not.

Being an ambitious and energetic Cardinal Sign, Capricorn has an enormous ability to use these Earthy qualities in a productive capacity. If you have planets next door in the humanitarian Signs of Aquarius or Sagittarius, you just might lean toward wanting to do something to help save this crazy world, or some portion thereof.

You can bring much that is positive to a relationship. Your strong personality and practical nature gives a man the feeling that he can trust and depend on you. With your natural grace and charm, and your dignified aura (not to mention that fabulous wit), he would be proud to show you off anywhere.

You don't need boring, uninspired men who lack your brand of ambition, no matter how attractive they might be or how much money they may have (obviously inherited money if they lack ambition); there are more important issues. As the most ambitious and accomplishment-oriented lady of the entire zodiac, you absolutely must have a man of a similar nature. By the way, if you have major influence in the Martian Elements of Fire, you will have an even greater urge for accomplishment.

For this reason, my first choices for you would be an ambitious fellow Capricorn (though this relationship could be a competitive one) or a Taurus with enough Cardinal influence. Any man without a planet—preferably a major one—in Capricorn could not possibly have your unique slant on things: your sharp, accurate, literal, irreverent interpretation of life. A problem area to watch out for with Taurus: it is a Fixed Sign (Taurus the Bull!), and he can be bent on his own point of view. However, if he has a balanced chart, this man will make a devoted, caring, protective, and lovable mate. The Virgo man is very kind, gentle, and sensitive. He is among the most family-oriented and devoted of the zodiac, but romantic he's not.

What about Air Sign men? Here we have good news and bad news. As the other mental Element, Air has definite compatibility potential. The Air Sign men will see the subject of emotion from a similar viewpoint. However, Air is a different type of thinking: abstract and analytical. An Air Sign man would need enough Earth influence in his chart to make him more practical and down to earth.

Libra, being a Cardinal Sign, is probably my first choice of the Air Sign men. A Libra man tends to be indecisive, but he does have your Cardinal ambition (if he can ever decide what to do with it!), and he has the best disposition of the Air Signs. He will be the most relationship-prone of the Air Sign men, as Libra is in the Western Hemisphere.

An Aquarius man would be my next choice; this Sign being right next door to Capricorn, you might have interchanging planets. You will respect this man's mind. He is perhaps the most brilliant of the zodiac and Gemini's free spirit might be just the thing for Capricorn's serious side. Gemini men are intelligent, communicative, quick-witted, and idealistic. A Capricorn woman could help to bring reality to his idealism.

While neither of the Feeling Elements of Fire or Water is emotionally compatible with you, Capricorn with a Fire Sign man epitomizes the clash of Mental and Emotional Elements. With Capricorn's more dignified, reserved approach to emotion, the intense emotionality of the Fire or Water man is particularly negative. You will think he lacks practicality, is irresponsible, and is emotionally immature. And, as far as his opinion of you, do you want a man who feels that you are too logical, practical, and emotionally removed?

By the way, once you find this wonderful man who is very Earthy, romantic, ambitious, and sensitive to your needs, do not scare him off with one of the your most prevalent traits. Capricorns are notorious for always having to "set the record straight" regarding everything! Bless your heart, it's a nasty job, but someone has to do it! Part of this urge has to do with this Sign's need to be seen as an authority or expert in something, whether it is your career, a hobby, or Trivial Pursuit—you love to excel. But I think the basic desire stems from your capacity to see things accurately, and you just cannot resist letting others in on your "correct" interpretations! And, you know what? Very often you are right!

THE AIR SIGN WOMEN: LIBRA, GEMINI, AQUARIUS

Aɪʀ Tʏᴘᴇ ᴏꜰ Tʜɪɴᴋɪɴɢ: Abstract, Analytical, Idealistic, Independent, Intellectual, Futuristic, Objective, Romantic.

Gᴇɴᴅᴇʀ: Masculine (Martian, confrontive).

More direct and outspoken than the feminine Elements of Water and Earth.

Emotionally compatible only with Air and Earth men.

The Element of Air, like Fire, is very romantic and idealistic. But, unlike Fire, Air is not given to frequent emotional displays. While both Fire and Water Sign women thrive on "feeling" their feelings, the Air lady wishes to remain just that: a lady! Expressing one's feelings in too emotional a manner may seem quite uncivilized to Air. Those with very high Air influence can literally become physically ill when confronted with highly emotional situations over which they feel a lack of control. Air Sign women (and men) like to be in control of their emotions, and have a need to remain (or at least appear) cool, calm, and collected. And this is definitely the Element to carry it off! Air, with its extreme sensitivity, instinctive graciousness, and innate sense of class radiates elegance and grace.

This Air brand of Thinking is intellectually creative—capable of flash insight unequaled by the other Elements. Air is the world of ideas, of possibilities, always looking to the future. If you have more than two major planets in Air, some may view you as an impractical dreamer. The Air Signs also have great perspective, possessing the ability to view ideas and values outside of their own realm with great objectivity. However, when there are too many major planets in the Air Signs, all of that objectivity may tend to get lost due to an excess of idealism and perfectionism.

Air woman, you are ultrasensitive, with a gentle, almost distant quality by which men are very taken. Speaking of men, you like those who are intellectual and educated—men with class! The man in your life needs to be very together, very stable. This will help offset your feelings of insecurity which, to a greater or lesser extent, are basic to the nature of Air.

Your own Element of Air would ideally be the best potential match for real emotional intimacy (if his chart reflects a balance of Elements). An Air Sign man would understand your need for emotional space and not take it as a rejection, realizing that it is simply your nature. He would also sympathize with your inclination to analyze and dissect your emotions so that you can organize and alphabetize them; after all, he does the same thing! What better way to control them? However, an Air Sign man, particularly one with too much Air emphasis, may always want to be in control of everything—including you. Your extremely independent side will not appreciate this. A man with very high Air influence is not only controlling, but can also be opinionated, domineering, and judgmental (though it may indeed be beautifully camouflaged by his sweet, gracious Air personality). These men suffer from "overly masculine" behavior when they have too many planets in the Martian Elements of Air or Fire (see Chapter 6: The Male Chauvinist, Astrologically Defined). Air Sign men can also be ultra-touchy about any kind of criticism. And what he considers criticism may be nothing more than helpful suggestions on your part.

Also emotionally compatible with Air is the other mental Element of Earth (Taurus, Virgo, Capricorn). Since Air has a rather distracted or scattered quality, a reliable, practical Earth Sign man could be helpful in terms of providing a sense of stability. I therefore often recommend these men over your own Element of Air. If an Earth man has too many planets in the Earth Signs, he could be too practical and down-to-earth for an Air Sign woman, unless you also have several planets in Earth. He must have enough Air to be able to share your romantic, analytical, futuristic Air brand of thinking.

Now let's take a look at the Fire Sign men. These fiery men are a definite clash for Air women (see Chapter 3: The Clash Between Thinkers and Feelers). You may indeed find yourself attracted to Fire, which shares many of the same qualities as Air; you are both idealistic, futuristic, intuitive, creative, and romantic. However, you must remember that these men possess a brand of intense emotionality that is very different from your more cautious, reserved approach to emotion. Your Element of Air is the most sensitive to a show of harsh or intense emotions. Fire Sign men with too many planets in the Fire or Air Signs have a problem with overly masculine behavior (aggressive, demanding, opinionated, perfectionistic, controlling).

What about the Water Sign men (Cancer, Scorpio, Pisces)? Again, we have the same emotional clash as with Fire Sign men. You will be fundamentally uncomfortable interacting with the deep, brooding emotional nature of these highly emotionally sensitive men. As with the Fire Sign men, these men need a brand of emotional connection that will make you feel anxious and pressured. I can hear you thinking, "But I am a very emotional person!" Yes, you may have many very emotional factors in your chart, but that doesn't change the fact that, with your Sun Sign being a Mental one, you are basically not comfortable with emotion the way a Feeler (Fire or Water) is. Ironically, you often become emotional *because* you are not comfortable with feeling your feelings! Incidentally, these Water Sign men can appear to be on your wavelength due to their ultrasensitive nature, seemingly so similar to your own. However, their brand of sensitivity is highly emotional, while yours is more mental.

And remember, the man in your life must be not only very self-confident, but very independent in order to understand and respect your immense need for freedom and independence. You become very uncomfortable when anyone infringes upon that need.

The Gemini Woman: Air Thinking Sign
(May 22–June 21)

ELEMENT: Air (an abstract, idealistic brand of thinking).

Independent, Futuristic, Analytical, Idealistic, Communicative, Romantic, Changeable, Restless, Curious.

GENDER: Masculine (Martian, confrontive).

EASTERN HEMISPHERE

A MUTABLE SIGN: Flexible and changeable.

Emotionally compatible only with Air and Earth sign men.

Gemini is the ultimate communicator. No strong, silent Gary Cooper types for you! You need a man who will talk to you, and talk, and talk! You are not into idle chit-chat; you like to analyze life's problems and share your findings with the world. Gemini is ruled by Mercury, the planet governing communication. You are extremely bright and quick-witted. You need a man who can keep up with you, mentally and physically. You can change your mind, your mood, and your desires with Mercurial speed, hence The Twins as the symbol for Gemini. Few men can keep up with you. As soon as they think they've got you figured out, there you go again, off in another direction. But, of course, all of this is part of your considerable charm.

Which men of the zodiac will not bore you to tears? Your own Element of Air with its impulsive restless spirit is the best possibility. Libra is my first choice. Of the Air Signs, this man will be the most concerned about your needs, the most gracious, and the most ambitious. Your own Sign of Gemini will relate to your changeability and need for variety. However, I would like to see one or both of you with major planets in the Earth or Fixed Signs to stabilize Air's naturally scattered energies. As far as the Air Sign of Aquarius goes, these men are very charismatic and brilliant; you may be very attracted to them. However, this is a Fixed Sign, and he would need enough Mutable influence to add flexibility to his thinking.

The Element also on your emotional wavelength is the other mental Element of Earth (Taurus, Virgo, Capricorn). Actually, an Earth Sign man with the right chart could be better than your own Element of Air, due to the problems found with so many of the Air Sign men. However, this Earth brand of thinking is reality-based, logical, and practical. Therefore, for real compatibility his chart should have at least one major planet in the Air Signs to give him your analytical, futuristic brand of thinking.

My first choice of the Earth Sign men for Gemini would be Capricorn. They are among the wittiest and the mentally sharpest of the zodiac—and, oddly enough, among the most serious in spite of their sense of humor. The Earth Sign of Taurus is certainly a possibility; though there could be difficulty if you possess the typical restless Gemini spirit, as he is not too crazy about change. With Taurus being the Sign right next door to Gemini, there might be some planet interchanges that would help with compatibility. And as for Virgo, you two could talk all night, with both Signs ruled by Mercury. These gentle, kindhearted men can make thoughtful and devoted husbands.

You may find yourself drawn to Water Sign men (Cancer, Scorpio, Pisces) because of their great sensitivity, which you may view as being similar to your own. But remember, his is a very different brand of sensitivity. Water men have a super-sensitive brand of emotion. While you make decisions after analyzing the facts, he bases decisions on how he feels. Water men need from you a style of relating and a brand of emotional interaction that is foreign to your Thinking Element of Air.

What about the Fire men (Aries, Leo, Sagittarius)? They are off limits—a definite no-no! Unless you mean men who work at the fire station, we are going to have to rule out these gentlemen for Air women. Unfortunately, you will probably find yourself attracted to Fire Sign men because of the similarities between Air and Fire; both of these Elements are romantic, idealistic, creative, and futuristic. I hope you take my advice and stick with Air men who are also all of these things! If you find yourself feeling tempted to become involved with a Fire Sign man, take another look at Chapter 6 on the dysfunctional behavior of so many of these Fire Sign men and see if you don't change your mind. When these men have too many planets in the masculine Element of Fire, they can be very controlling, spoiled, demanding, and aggressive.

When you have finally found your "one and only," do not make the mistake that many Gemini women tend to make: don't think that because you are in love, you will not find other men attractive. It's just that fickle Gemini thing; don't let it make you crazy. A Gemini woman can be genuinely in love, and still have a strong need to flirt with other men. It is simply your nature; it doesn't have to mean anything! Do not stay in a relationship with a man who cannot fully understand and accept this aspect of your personality. Obviously, a Gemini woman needs a man with a great deal of self-confidence and maturity so that he does not make life miserable for both of you with childish whining about how you wouldn't flirt with other men if you really loved him. Gemini loves to flirt, and you need a man who will not only understand your flirtatious nature, but who will flirt with you too!

And, remember, Ms. Sociability, don't always talk his ear off! He will be charmed by your personality and intrigued by your verbal skills, but leave him wanting, just a little!

The Libra Woman: Air Thinking Sign
(September 24–October 23)

ELEMENT: Air (an Abstract, idealistic brand of thinking).

Independent, Diplomatic, Artistic, Romantic, Cooperative, Paradoxical.

GENDER: Masculine (Martian, confrontive).

WESTERN HEMISPHERE

A CARDINAL SIGN: Energetic and ambitious.

Emotionally compatible only with Air and Earth sign men.

Libra is Ms. Indecisive. Being as fickle, flirtatious, and independent as you Libra ladies are, it can be very difficult for you to give up all the other men for only one!

But given the fact that Libra is the house of partnership, it is a choice that, once made, should feel very comfortable. Of all the Signs in the zodiac, Libra needs to feel that, once a decision has been made, it is the right one. You do not deal very well with stress. You can have a hard enough time making up your mind in the first place, but to then feel that it was not the right decision—well, there you are right back in the thick of it, with all those conflicting thoughts to deal with all over again. Libras are made very uneasy by complicated emotional issues. When it comes to deciding if a man is right for you, try to ignore your brain and feel it with your heart!

Venus, the planet of love and beauty, rules the Sign of Libra, giving you an unusual eye for beauty and symmetry. You have an extremely romantic and poetic nature; you love the whole idea of being courted: the flowers, the gifts, the candlelight dinners. The ultimate would be a man who writes you poetry! Only a Libra lady with a very high Earth influence might be happy with a man who was not a true romantic.

By the way, in spite of your natural Libra class, style, and elegance, you are really quite a paradox—the steel hand in a velvet glove. There is great strength behind your delicate demeanor. This most gracious and charming lady of the zodiac can go for the jugular if she indulges the repressed anger for which her Sign is known.

Air is very idealistic and perfectionistic. I know it can be difficult for you to accept less than perfection, to deal with things that are imbalanced—after all, Libra (The Scales) is always seeking balance—but since there is such a shortage of perfect men out there, this penchant for perfection could really hinder finding a mate.

Let's take a look at the Signs that will be the most likely to meet Libra's need for harmonious romance. If he has a good balance of Elements, a fellow Air Sign would be ideal. Of the three Air men, unquestionably the best choice is a fellow Libra, who will share not only your sunny disposition, but also your Western Hemisphere focus on relationships. Gemini, though in the Eastern Hemisphere (less concerned with the needs of others), is at least flexible, being a Mutable Sign. And, ruled by the planet Mercury, these men are very communicative. They are also restless and changeable: you'll never be bored! Aquarius is Mr. Personality; these men are brilliant and can be exceptionally funny. If you are highly creative and have humanitarian instincts, you will have that much more in common with the Aquarian man.

Though you are theoretically most compatible with these men of your own Element, the Air Sign men can have problems. As bright, gracious, and mesmerizing as they can be one minute, they can be very emotionally removed the next.

Because of the problem with some Air Sign men being too Martian, I sometimes prefer the other Mental Element of Earth for Libra women (Taurus, Virgo, Capricorn). However, ideally he would have Air influence in his chart to give him the sensitivity you require, as well as your brand of analytical, abstract, and futuristic Thinking. Of the Earth Signs, my first choice is Taurus. Like Libra, it is ruled by Venus, the planet of love and beauty. A Taurus man particularly loves the beauty and grandeur of this earth. He makes a loyal and devoted companion. A Capricorn is an excellent possibility if he has at least one major planet in Air. Capricorn, like Libra, is an ambitious Cardinal Sign. You will both have the desire to start many new projects. Virgo is my last choice for a romantic Libra lady, only because these men tend to be the least romantic men of the zodiac. But if there is enough influence in the romantic Fire and Air Signs in his chart, this could be a great match. Virgo is also a Mutable Sign, and therefore flexible. Being located next door to Libra, you might have interchanging planets.

The Fire Signs (Aries, Leo, Sagittarius) are emotionally disastrous for Air Sign women. They are cut from a very different emotional cloth. To fully understand the ways in which these intensely emotional men are incompatible with Libra women, see Chapter 3: The Clash Between Thinkers and Feelers. A Fire Sign man could really disrupt the Libra need for peace and tranquillity. He will see you as aloof and emotionally distant, while you will think he is too impulsive and lacking in emotional control.

As far as Water Sign men are concerned, they are definitely not on your emotional wavelength. Water men possess a deep, brooding brand of emotionality that really requires a Water or Fire Sign woman who is comfortable with their emotional nature. You may indeed be drawn to these men in terms of their sensitivity, but remember that it is a very different brand of sensitivity. At worst, he will feel that you are too analytical and emotionally distant. You will think that he is an insecure, emotional baby.

For a romantic Libra lady, who loves to be in love, to be unhappy in romance is a sad thing indeed, especially with so many gentlemen who are eagerly awaiting your approval. Unfortunately, a Libra lady will often make the mistake of staying with the wrong man who does not deserve a date with her, much less a life. If you are in a relationship that you truly know is wrong, dig deep into that Libra inner strength and find a way out; you deserve better, you deserve the best!

The Aquarius Woman: Air Thinking Sign
(January 21–February 19)

ELEMENT: Air (an abstract, idealistic brand of thinking).

Independent, Altruistic, Brilliant, Highly Original, Humanitarian, Unpredictable.

GENDER: Masculine (Martian, confrontive).

EASTERN HEMISPHERE

A FIXED SIGN: Determined and persistent.

Emotionally compatible only with Air and Earth Sign men.

Aquarius is one of the brightest ladies of the zodiac! The man in your life had better be equally intelligent, with your Air brand of flash insight and your quick, abstract analytical thinking process. Born to challenge and discover, you have a mind that works like radar. Regardless of whatever other fine attributes he may possess, any man whose mind is not as sharp as yours will not only bore you, but you will be unable to muster the proper respect for him. The man in your life also needs to share your humanitarian nature. Your Sign is matched only by Sagittarius in terms of its desire to help others, to save the world. And Aquarius and Sagittarius are also the two most fiercely independent Signs. Your man would have to understand your extreme need for freedom, especially the freedom to explore your many friendships which are so imperative to every Aquarian. He does not have to be as social as you are, but he needs to have great understanding for your needs in this area. And, almost above all else, Aquarius has a tremendous need to be seen accurately and appreciated.

What man shares and understands all these Aquarius traits? A fellow Air Sign! An Air Sign man will have your unique brand of ultrasensitivity, being very thoughtful and considerate of others.

My first recommendation would be the Sign of Libra. Being in the Western Hemisphere, he is more relationship-oriented and more giving and caring than either Aquarius or Gemini. Libra men are terrific and make wonderful, loyal mates. A fellow Aquarian, without too much total Fixed influence, could be very compatible. These men are highly intelligent and very charismatic. But the average Gemini man might make you a little nuts with his restless and changeable nature. They are also very controlling and the most self-directed of the Air Signs.

The other emotionally compatible Element for Aquarius is Earth (Taurus, Virgo, Capricorn). But bear in mind that, although you both handle emotion in a similar fashion, Air and Earth are two very different brands of thinking. Air is abstract, analytical, and futuristic; Earth functions with logic and reason in the here and now. The Capricorn man could be particularly compatible. Your Signs are next to each other, and it is therefore likely that you will have planets in each other's Signs. You will also appreciate this man's exceptional thinking process—a combination of common sense, awareness, and intelligence unmatched by any other Sign. Taurus, the most romantic of the Earth Sign men could be a very good match. But you are both Fixed Signs. One or both of you had better have major planets in the Mutable Signs to add flexibility to your relationship. Not nearly as romantic as Taurus, the Mutable Virgo man has many fine qualities. He is without question the most genuinely loving and caring of the Earth Signs. (The only other Mental Sign man as dear and gentle as Virgo is Libra.)

We can virtually rule out six of the twelve Signs: the Fire and Water Signs. The War Between the Signs is clearly illustrated in the clash between your Element of Air and the Fire and Water Signs. These highly emotional men make Aquarius women uneasy with what you would view as emotional demands and pressure. This clash between the Mental and Emotional Signs makes it impossible to build true emotional intimacy between a man and a woman. There is an enormous gap in emotional wavelength (see Chapter 3).

This emotional gap is a real problem when it comes to the intensely emotional Fire Sign men to whom Air women are invariably attracted! You will be drawn to the traits that Air and Fire have in common. Like you, he will be creative, futuristic, intuitive, and romantic. However, his very emotional nature is not something that Air or Earth Sign women can ultimately relate to. Your innately more reserved and controlled approach to the processing of your emotions clashes with his more intense way of expressing his feelings. And, speaking of emotion, a Fire Sign man with too much Fire or Air can have the emotional makeup of a child. He can be aggressive and demanding in expressing his impatience when things do not go according to *his* game plan.

What about the Water Sign men (Cancer, Scorpio, Pisces)? Though you will be drawn to the sensitivity of Water men, remember that these men are on a different emotional wavelength. You make decisions about your life more as a result of thought and analysis; these men make decisions based on how they feel. With it being their nature to give priority to their emotional needs, Air Sign women sometimes view them as emotional babies. He will feel that you don't love him, don't care enough about his needs. You will never be able to achieve the level of emotional intimacy with a Water Sign man that you can with an Air or Earth Sign man.

When you do run across Mr. Right, please don't make some of the typical Aquarian mistakes. You can be so idealistic and such a perfectionist when it comes to romance that you may rule out a man who could be truly wonderful for you. With Aquarius being a Fixed Sign, you may also lack flexibility and open-mindedness unless you have at least two major planets in the Mutable (flexible) Signs. Another thing to bear in mind is that your Sign is in the Eastern Hemisphere. If you have several additional planets in this Hemisphere, you may be so emotionally independent that you need to work on being more tuned in to the wishes of your mate. Sometimes just a little extra gesture can make all the difference. Mesmerize him with your delightful, charming Aquarius personality, and he will be yours forever!

14

The Thinking Sign Men: Earth and Air

THE EARTH SIGN MEN: TAURUS, VIRGO, CAPRICORN

EARTH BRAND OF THINKING: Practical, Down-to-Earth, Literal, Detail-Minded, Conventional, Cautious, Realistic.

GENDER: Feminine (Venusian, nonconfrontive).

Emotionally compatible only with Earth and Air women.

These men are from Venus, at least in terms of their feminine Earth Sun Sign. With other major planets in the feminine (Venusian) Elements of Earth and Water, they will be more on a woman's wavelength. However, there can be a problem with Earth Sign men being too Venusian (nonconfrontive, too giving to others, etc.) if there are not enough major planets in the Martian Elements of Air and Fire.

The Earth Sign man is unquestionably the best choice for an Earth Sign woman. These dependable, reasonable, logical, practical men share your down-to-earth approach to romance. This is not to say that he will never give you flowers or expensive gifts but, unlike a Fire Sign man, he will not be inclined to indulge in extravagances that he cannot afford. This will be to the liking of most Earth Sign women, who will not be thrilled by a man whose idea of creative money management could involve spending the mortgage payment on a trip to the Bahamas! The Earth Sign man will not provide you with all the romantic gestures that the romantic Fire or Air man (or sensitive Water man) will, but he will be more inclined to provide you with security. For most Earth ladies, that is more important!

These Earth men approach life and love with a certain practicality that will be most appreciated by a fellow "Earthling!" While the Water or Air couples are writing each other touching, sensitive poems, and the Fire couples are spending money on expensive candlelight dinners, the Earth couple will be contemplating the renewal of their *Money* magazine subscription while re-tiling the kitchen.

I even prefer these grounded Earth Sign men for many Air Sign women over their own Element of Air. There are two reasons for this. First, Air Sign men can have problems with being too Martian. Second, the Earth Sign men can bring emotional stability to the Air Sign women who need grounding. However, bear in mind that Air is abstract and analytical and focuses on the future. Earth is a more practical brand of thinking and focuses on the here and now. In order for an Earth Sign man to be intuitive enough for an Air Sign woman, his chart should have one or two major planets in the Air Signs. And his overall Earth emphasis should not be so high that he would bore the restless, impulsive Air woman.

The Earth Sign men are highly emotionally incompatible with the Water and Fire Signs. These women have too emotional a nature for the more pragmatic Earth man to feel comfortable with them in an intimate relationship. These men do not relate well to too much emotional display, be it negative or positive; they simply operate on a more mental level. And I must warn you, if you are a Water or Fire Sign woman who needs to be understood emotionally, this Earth man will want everything to make sense, to be logical. If he thinks you are being illogical, he will tend to dismiss your feelings. The more subtle nuances of communication, which are particularly important to a Water Sign woman, often escape him entirely. Because he will be prone to look at the facts, you may often be left with the impression that your feelings do not matter. It is not necessarily that they don't matter to him; it is simply that he doesn't really understand them! And when he attempts to do so by reviewing and analyzing everything, he will sometimes conclude that your feelings just do not hold any weight when measured against the facts! He will tend to miss the important point that you are entitled to your feelings even if, due to his more logical outlook, he doesn't relate to them. It can be quite fascinating to observe the Earth Sign man trying to explain away your feelings to you: "Why are you so upset about losing your job when you knew it was coming weeks ago?" Any attempt to explain to him that your feelings are not erased by the fact that you had advance notice will fall on emotionally deaf ears. These men are more at home with facts than with feelings.

This is the man who will proudly present his lady love with a beautiful new food processor for their anniversary—*and* that trash compactor she's been wanting (after all, it is their twentieth anniversary). If this lady is a Water Sign, he will probably spend the remainder of the day wondering why she seems less than completely thrilled with these lovely, practical tokens of his love. If she is a slightly more romantically-oriented Fire Sign, he might wish that he had given her a little something in gold to go along with those useful appliances. However, another Earth Sign might find these thoughtful, practical gifts to be just the right gesture.

The typical Earth Sign man will be self-sufficient, trustworthy, reasonable, reliable, and probably somewhat conservative. He also has a strong need for productivity and accomplishment, especially Capricorn. Earth men generally possess good common sense, and are very detail-minded and literal (Capricorn and Virgo, more than Taurus). Earth likes familiarity and consistency; he has a very real need for security (particularly

Virgo), and finds life's tendency to shift and change rather distasteful (Taurus really hates it!). You can see how there could be a slight clash with a spontaneous Fire Sign woman.

If he has too many planets in the Earth Signs, there can be some problems. Needless to say, all of the traits discussed above will be even more pronounced. This type of chart would produce an individual who wants what he wants when he wants it—often without considering anyone else. More than three major planets in the Earth Signs can also make a man very demanding that things be done according to his plans—and he will invariably have a plan!

These men can be extremely logical and practical about everything. Of the four Elements, Earth is the least emotional and the least romantic. (You will notice that I refer to the Element of Earth; not every Earth Sign man is totally unemotional and unromantic.) The more planets he has in the romantic Elements of Fire or Air, the more romantic his nature. However, even with enough Fire and Air to make him more romantic—or key planets in the Water Signs to make him more sensitive—an Earth Sign man is an Earth Sign man. Earth is a Mental Element and therefore emotionally incompatible with an Emotional Sign woman (Fire or Water). Even if he has Venus, the planet of love, in an Emotional Element, it will not change the fact that he is fundamentally uncomfortable with the subject of emotionality. He approaches anything related to feelings in a totally different way than an emotional Sun Sign individual.

Eastern Hemisphere Earth Signs: Taurus, Capricorn
Less relationship-oriented
Less concerned with the needs of others

Any of the more self-centered aspects of the Element of Earth will be magnified in the Eastern Hemisphere, since the Eastern Signs are more focused on themselves and less concerned with your needs.

Western Hemisphere Earth Sign: Virgo
More relationship-oriented
More concerned with the needs of others

Being in the Western Hemisphere makes Virgo the most relationship-oriented of the three Signs—the most agreeable, the least self-centered. Virgo is one of the most devoted of all the Signs. They possess a much greater level of sensitivity; and have a far more gentle nature than the other two Earth Signs.

The Taurus Man: Earth Thinking Sign
(April 21–May 21)

ELEMENT: Earth (a logical, practical brand of thinking).

Reliable, Patient, Possessing Great Fortitude, Stubborn, Sensuous, Possessive, Materialistic, Self-Indulgent.

GENDER: Feminine (Venusian, nonconfrontive).

EASTERN HEMISPHERE

A FIXED SIGN: Determined and persistent.

Emotionally compatible only with Earth and Air women.

Is the Taurus man always stubborn, bent on his point of view, and difficult to get along with? Nonsense! As long as everything goes his way, he can be absolutely charming and very pleasant indeed! While Taurean men can be warm, caring, loyal, generous, and devoted, they can also be the most possessive, demanding, obstinate men you will ever meet. Whether an individual Taurus man leans in one direction or the other will depend on how much additional Earth or Fixed influence he has elsewhere in his chart, and whether he has a problem with too many planets in the Martian Elements of Fire or Air. This high masculine influence will make a Taurus man extremely bent on having things his own way.

At their worst, these men can be incredibly inflexible—pigheaded, actually. It amazes me how some women let them get away with this absurd behavior, saying, " What can you expect? He's Taurus The Bull!" Well, speaking of *bull!* What you ought to be able to expect is an emotional grown-up who doesn't demand that everything be done his way! No one need use their astrological energies as an excuse to treat others badly. I would like to see him have a minimum of two, and preferably three, major planets in the adaptable Mutable Signs (Gemini, Virgo, Sagittarius, Pisces). It would be particularly desirable if this flexible influence involved the functional planets of Mercury (think), Venus (love), or Mars (act).

Incidentally, there is some good news regarding the instincts that produce the infamous Taurus stubbornness. The combination of his being an Earth and a Fixed Sign creates a man who is a pillar of strength and is among the most supportive of the Signs. The evolved Taurus man will use this amazing tenacity and determination to achieve his goals rather than impersonating a stubborn child. Many Taurus men simply need the discipline they never received in their early childhood—or since! You might begin by enlightening him as to just how important it is to be more open to another's needs and feelings. I urge you not to let one of the Taurus-the-Bully types think he can put his foot down and flat-out refuse to consider any further input. You simply need to tell him that this level of inflexibility is not something you are able to process. Let him know that all of his "pawing the ground and snorting" does not impress you in the least!

If Mr. Taurus has an overall balanced chart and enough planets in the Western Hemisphere to make him genuinely concerned about your needs and feelings, this man can make the best mate of the zodiac for Earth and Air Sign women. His basic nature is incredibly loving and devoted, and his courage, vitality, and robust sense of humor could charm you into wondering what you ever did without him. He can be incredibly affectionate. Taurus is the most sensuous of the Signs—gentle, calm, considerate, kind, thoughtful, and faithful. His steady, strong, stable, solid character can make a woman feel very emotionally secure. His patience and protectiveness can make him a wonderful father.

Incidentally, add to the Taureans' love of nature their love of possessions and fine things, and you have the Sign that would most enjoy a magnificent country estate. We would then have one contented bull!

The Earth Sign women would usually be the most emotionally compatible with these men. Air Sign women possess an entirely different brand of thinking (futuristic, abstract, and analytical). Because Taurus is ruled by Venus (the planet of love and beauty), the Taurus man will identify more readily with the Air woman's idealistic, romantic nature than will the other Earth Sign men. However, there could be a problem if an Air Sign woman has additional major planets in the Air Signs, as she will possess a brand of sensitivity that a Taurus man might have a problem relating to unless he has solid emphasis in the Air Signs. Another possible problem area for the very independent Air Sign woman might be the Taurus gentleman's tendency for possessiveness. Needless to say, this would not go over well with a Fire Sign woman either!

The Emotional Sign women (Fire and Water) are a major mismatch with the Earth Sign men, though they might feel otherwise when meeting a Taurus man who excels in the courtship department. Of all the Thinking Signs, the Taurus gentleman, who often has courting down to a science, may strike a real emotional chord in a Fire or Water Sign lady. With his Sign being ruled by Venus, the Taurus man almost has an obsession for the grandeur of nature. He may impress you with a picnic on a cliff overlooking the ocean or an impromptu champagne helicopter ride at dawn. However, if you are a Fire or Water Sign woman, you must remember that he operates in a very different way when it comes to emotions; unlike you, his emotions are thought out and controlled. He will never make you feel that he really understands you emotionally. His bold, exciting courtship gestures are definitely on your romantic wavelength, but unfortunately he is not on your emotional wavelength! A Taurus will be unable to fulfill your need for emotional connection on a regular basis or in the way that you need.

By the way, Taureans often have a wonderful sense of humor—just one more thing to initially sweep you Emotional Sun Sign women off your feet! The fact is that these men can be among the most incredibly charming of the zodiac. There is just something about most Taurean men, who have graciousness down to a science, that is adorable and endearing.

The Virgo Man: Earth Thinking Sign (August 24–September 23)

ELEMENT: Earth (a logical, practical brand of thinking).

Conscientious, Discriminating, Methodical, Thoughtful, Helpful, Kind, Devoted.

GENDER: Feminine (Venusian, nonconfrontive).

WESTERN HEMISPHERE

A MUTABLE SIGN: Flexible and changeable.

Emotionally compatible only with Earth and Air women.

Virgo is not the Sign for you if you are yearning for dynamic displays of undying love and adoration, demonstrated with wild abandon. Hardworking, conscientious, patient, gentle, considerate, and understanding he is; a man to dynamically and impulsively sweep you off your feet he is not! I am describing the traits of the Sign of Virgo. This will not apply quite as much to a Virgo man with other influences that offset the typically modest, conservative qualities of this sweet, emotionally reserved man. There is sometimes a strong enough in-

fluence in the Fire Signs to make a Virgo man more spontaneous and romantic in his approach to love. However, even a
Virgo with strong Fire influence is still a Thinker, who is fundamentally not comfortable with too much emotion and
therefore highly incompatible with Feelers (Fire and Water
Sign Women).

The average Virgo man is simply too methodical and analytical to fall head over heels for anyone. It is just not his nature! I
can hear you Fire women thinking, "Now I know why those
Virgo men, who I *knew* were attracted to me, just couldn't manage to express it in a way I could relate to!" Being innately more
detached from his feelings, his way would involve meticulously
dissecting a potential relationship prior to making any emotional decisions. Does that sound odd? "Emotional decision"?
This man doesn't react with emotional impulsiveness the way a
Fire or Water man would; he literally (and he is also very literal) decides what his emotions are. He seems to be thinking
his feelings, rather than feeling them. He reviews and contem-
plates things until he feels safe about deciding to slowly enter
into a relationship—that is, provided that all of the data and
input appear to warrant such an action! If this approach
sounds dreadful to you, then you are not the right woman for
this man anyway. The typical Earth or Air Sign woman would
not find this cautious approach to love to be so foreign. Quite
the opposite, she would probably find a more hasty, emotional
approach to be stressful or maybe even unthinkable.

A Virgo man is definitely not a possibility for an emotional
Fire or Water Sign woman. A Virgo man would not be emotionally expressive enough for her romantic nature. Virgo is probably
the worst possible choice of the entire zodiac for any Fire Sign
woman. There is a very strong innate emotional clash between
Virgo and Fire. One of the reasons for the level of this clash is
the fact that, of all the Signs, Virgo is the most ultrasensitive
to criticism—or anything even remotely resembling criticism.
Fire has a communication style that invariably makes Virgo feel

pressured, anxiety-ridden, or criticized. Virgo people can be virtually paranoid about the "C" word! There are other reasons for
this extreme clash. While Fire tends to thrive on change and spontaneity, the Sign of Virgo is fundamentally allergic to that type of
functioning. Virgo men do not exactly relate to unpredictability.
They instinctively prefer that things be planned and well thought
out. (Do these guys sound like a clash with Fire or what?)

Anything in a state of disarray can really upset a Virgo. Not all
men of this Sign are necessarily super-neatniks when it comes to
closets and drawers, but every Virgo has a need for controlled
emotions and a desire for well-ordered relationships.

Virgo is probably tied with Scorpio for the Most Nonconfrontive Award! Being a Thinking Sign, which is basically
uncomfortable with emotion, makes them resistant to exploring
issues that will bring about emotional discussions. Forget sharing their feelings with you; they often do not know what they
feel! Any man with even one major planet in Virgo would need
to really work at being more direct and candid about his needs
and feelings. These men can become extremely stressed by their
pent-up emotions. Anyone with a major Virgo influence can be
prone to high blood pressure as a result of keeping everything
inside. If their life becomes chaotic and disorganized, they have
a need to imagine that everything is fine—all structured and
orderly. Incidentally, this is one more cause of major incompatibility with Fire Sign women. With Fire being the most
confrontive Element, these women can become extremely frustrated by men who are so unable to readily express their
feelings!

The evolved Virgo man with a balanced chart could be
among the most devoted, concerned, giving, thoughtful, caring, conscientious, discriminating, and genuinely gracious of
men. But bear in mind that while he loves you dearly, Virgo
being possibly the most unromantic Sign of all, he will generally not be one to openly display his feelings. And be prepared
to deal with his fretting; he loves to worry and fuss over things.

You might attempt to find ways to make his life as predictable as possible; remember, Virgo loves predictability!

The Capricorn Man: Earth Thinking Sign (December 22–January 20)

ELEMENT: Earth (a logical, practical brand of thinking).

Detail-Minded, Literal, Cautious, Conventional, Discriminating, Manipulative, Calculating.

GENDER: Feminine (Venusian, nonconfrontive).

EASTERN HEMISPHERE

A CARDINAL SIGN: Energetic and ambitious.

Emotionally compatible only with Earth and Air women.

Highly ambitious, accomplishment-oriented, calculating, manipulative, detail-minded, authoritarian, moody, overly serious, sometimes even austere—it is all true about the Capricorn man! But he is also very practical, logical, reliable, reasonable, trustworthy, considerate, dependable, and traditional. And he probably has an incredibly wry sense of humor; it comes from his natural inclination (unsurpassed by any other Sign) to look at the world, and the people in it, in terms of the ridiculous. Because he can approach a subject or situation with such pure unemotional logic, he can see things with an accuracy that is utterly unique to this Sign. You would have to get up very early in the morning to put anything over on a Capricorn. If he has Mercury (the brain of the chart) in Capricorn, you had better not go to bed in the first place! This guy hears the grass grow!

Capricorns are unquestionably the most ambitious of all the Signs. This energy comes from the fact that Capricorn is a Cardinal Sign. Cardinal is initiative, stamina, physical energy, and control. While Taurus may work hard to acquire more toys, and Virgo to be of service to others, Capricorn has a need to accomplish which is greater than any other Sign. This produces a man who seems to work for the sake of work, for the joy of accomplishment. Some of these men are driven for success, driven to experience—not only the satisfaction of achievement, but the control it produces. Capricorns are likely candidates to be workaholics. They also have an exceptional business sense, and are usually adept in financial matters. Capricorn will not only be your lover, but your financial advisor!

Some Capricorn men can appear cold or brusque in their mannerisms as a way of covering up their soft interior. They definitely have a gentle, considerate, thoughtful side. He is the most serious Sign of the zodiac; perhaps a photo finish with Scorpio. Capricorn men sometimes feel that the world is trying to catch them with their pants down. Some of them really need to lighten up!

A Capricorn man with a good balance of Elements could be wonderful indeed for a fellow thinking Sign; only Earth and Air women need apply! Capricorns can make excellent mates for Earth women, who share their down-to-earth approach to life and love, and for Air women who have at least a moderate influence in the Earth Signs. He would need a major planet or two in the Air Signs, to add that Air brand of thinking (abstract and analytical). Without Air or Water (the two most sensitive Elements), these men could be too cold and matter-of-fact—too practical and Earthy in their attitude, and too insensitive for a delicate Air Sign lady.

What about women of the Emotional Elements of Water and Fire? These women will find the Mental Sign Capricorn men to be too unemotional in their approach to love. Capricorns will give the Emotional Sign women the feeling that they are thinking their emotions rather than feeling them. If you are an Emotional Sign woman, whose very being requires that a man be emotionally responsive, you will never feel that this man really understands your emotional needs—never mind responding to them! However, because these men do have a thoughtful, considerate side to their personality, you Water or Fire women might assume that they are capable of being there for you emotionally in the manner you require. This, however, is not the case. He may indeed appear to be on your emotional wavelength, but in time it will become painfully obvious that he is not cut out of your emotional cloth. It will be virtually impossible for a Feeling Sign woman to really feel emotionally connected to this Thinking Sign man. You will ultimately come to realize that he finds your need for emotional connection to be stressful and confining. It would not be uncommon at this point for a Capricorn man to attempt to manipulate you into believing that it is your problem—that you are simply an overly emotional woman who is insecure and, therefore, too demanding. The bottom line is that it is impossible for an Emotional Sign woman to really feel loved by a man who does not understand and respond to her in terms of her emotional needs.

THE AIR SIGN MEN: GEMINI, LIBRA, AQUARIUS

AIR BRAND OF THINKING: Abstract, Analytical, Idealistic, Independent, Intellectual, Futuristic, Objective, Romantic.

GENDER: Masculine (Martian, confrontive).

Emotionally compatible only with Air and Earth women.

These men are definitely from Mars! Their masculine Fire Sun Sign makes them more Martian than men with Venusian (Water or Earth) Sun Signs. If an Air Sign man has two or more additional planets in the masculine Elements of Fire or Air, he will be a "Super-Martian." It is very important that a chart be balanced with major planets in the feminine Elements of Water and Earth to add the qualities of kindness, sensitivity, consideration, and understanding.

While there are some sane, wonderful, adult-functioning Aquarius, Gemini, and Libra men out there, they would unquestionably need to have many balanced chart factors to help offset some of the problem areas so often found in Air Sign men (more about that in a moment).

An Air Sign man, with his naturally sweet disposition and outgoing, friendly manner, can be very endearing. He is gracious, thoughtful, relationship-oriented, communicative, and curious—curious about you, perhaps—at least until something else catches this elusive, restless man's eye. He may indeed be very interested in *you,* but that does not necessarily mean that he will seriously pursue anything too quickly.

Here is where the Feeling Sign woman has a problem: she can't relate to a man who *thinks* about how he *feels;* she needs a man who feels what he feels and *acts* upon it! But Air Sign men operate on such an instinctively mental level, having a fear of too much intense emotion, that they simply are unable to participate in the brand of emotional responsiveness that is virtually a requirement for Feeling Sign women. While these men can be quite charming and engaging due to their natural flair for communication, they do not function emotionally in a way that will allow these women to feel loved.

If you are an Emotional Sign woman, please do not mistake their ultrasensitivity and romantic nature as having anything to do with being on your emotional wavelength! In terms of your emotional needs, an Air Sign man will, at best, make you feel that he doesn't truly understand how you feel; at worst, he could at times seem like a combination of a computer and a refrigerator. All the while, he will probably tell you that any communication gaps result from your being an overly emotional woman who doesn't comprehend the fact that men are not into all that "talking about how they feel" nonsense.

Due to his emotionally hesitant nature, things as a rule don't get off to a whirlwind start with an Air Sign man. Unlike a Fire Sign man, who will usually be immediately in touch with what he feels for you, the Air Sign man will approach things much more cautiously. Remember, he is not comfortable with emotion to begin with, and he is really not comfortable with the variety of emotion that may cause him to lose control; being in control is crucial for any man with major Air influence in his chart. He is going to need time to dissect and analyze his feelings for you before he acts on them. With his Sun Sign being in a Mental Element, he tends not to trust his feelings. After he has decided that you appear to be safe and nonthreatening, he has the capacity for very sweet, touching, romantic gestures.

A fellow Air or Earth woman will identify with this more cautious attitude and even appreciate it. This woman needs a man who monitors and controls his feelings and possesses a more analytical mind. Incidentally, for an Earth Sign woman, he would ideally have planets in her Element of Earth in order to relate to her more practical brand of thinking, and she would need to have planets in the Air Signs to better relate to his abstract, elusive brand of thinking.

There are other reasons why Fire and Water Sign women need to avoid Air Sign men. These men are so emotionally removed from the type of frequent display of feelings you require that building real emotional intimacy with them is almost impossible for you. The clash of these Elements is discussed in great detail in Chapter 3: The Clash Between Thinkers and Feelers. Feeling Sign women will not feel any real depth of emotional bonding and closeness with the Aquarius man. Fire and Water Sign women thrive on emotional connection, and a Fire Sign woman needs an emotionally intense brand of communication that the Mental Sign man will go out of his way to avoid.

Unfortunately, the powers-that-be play tricks on Fire Sign women when it comes to these Air Sign men. The Elements of Fire and Air are similar in many ways; they are both creative, idealistic, futuristic, and romantic. Why, then, are they so incompatible? Fire Sign women are all of these things on an emotional level, while Air Sign men are all of these things on a more mental level. You can talk all night long to an Air Sign man, and exchange thoughts and ideas, but it may not seem as though you have exchanged emotions; he talks about his feelings, you feel your feelings.

Air Sign men can also be deceptive for Water Sign women. Air is a very sensitive Element, as is Water, but Water's sensitivity is emotional; Air's mental sensitivity is very different indeed. Water Sign women may find themselves very attracted to these men who can be so gentle, gracious, polite, kind, and considerate. Water women may sometimes feel certain that any one of these Air men must be an exception to the Thinker-Feeler clash. Wrong! What he appears to be, or what he genuinely feels for you, is irrelevant because he operates on such a different wavelength. He is not able to give you the kind of emotional feedback that you need on a consistent basis.

One cannot use the courtship behavior of a Mental Sign man as any guideline to what living with this man would be like over a period of time. It is not a question of his attempting to deliberately deceive you in any way. Because I have said that these men, by and large, are unable to make you feel their love, I must clarify the point that in some cases they may temporarily do a decent job of it. Air Sign men specialize in communication. Add to this their gentle, romantic nature, and these men are sometimes initially capable of making you feel their feelings for you. This, however, has nothing to do with the fact that they will never really understand the nature of your emotional makeup and the scope of your emotional needs. Even if he were able to fundamentally grasp what those needs are, he would not truly understand them. It would make him feel uncomfortable, pressured, or anxiety-ridden to even be aware of your needs, much less attempt to meet them on a regular basis. His frustration, which results from his inability to meet your emotional needs, will invariably cause him to suddenly relate to you from his "emotional igloo." When he becomes upset, he can abandon you emotionally with anything from a distant attitude to conversation dripping with icicles.

Men with two or more major planets in the Air Signs are usually very disciplined (it's that control thing) and good at setting standards and sticking to them. Often they will also want to set standards for you and see that you stick to them. This is where you may want to set some standards of your own. However, ironically, if he has very high Air emphasis, he could be too vague, detached, and distracted to stick to anything (particularly if he is a Gemini, with their restlessness and changeability). And that could be the least of the trouble. If an Air Sign man also has major planets in either Air or Fire, he can have a problem with being too Martian. He can be exceptionally perfectionistic, judgmental, opinionated, demanding, self-centered, and controlling. Too much masculine influence in his chart gives him an overdose of Martian traits (see Chapter 5: Why Can't a Man Be More Like a Woman?).

The other problem with men who have too many planets in Air is that they are super-touchy about anything they view as criticism. This often involves nothing more than your pleasant presentation of handy relationship hints. Remember that being a Thinking Element, which is basically not comfortable with too much show of emotion, an additional dose of Air (more than two planets) can really make him anxious when things become too emotional. He may now demonstrate for your enjoyment that unique capacity for turning his cold Air on you when his mood changes. You would swear that someone had turned on the air-conditioner! All of that lovely, gentle, considerate Air personality that we talked about earlier is out the window! Air men can totally redefine "removed and aloof"! What hope, you ask, is there for men with high Air influence? Very little! His chart would need to have other balanced factors, and he would need to have had exceptionally good childhood influences.

Should you attempt to bring this impractical dreamer down to earth, he will be less than cooperative. Air equals freedom and independence. Heaven forbid that anyone should try to point out the error of his ways! He will feel as though you are trying to control him again, and that, of course, is totally unacceptable. When you take issue with his attitude, he may call it a fight, when it might only be a conversation with a slight increase in volume. Actually, if you are also an Air Sign or an Earth Sign, this can be very compatible in terms of "fighting style;" you also think that too much emotional display is uncivilized. You will both analyze the situation and determine whether the benefits of having this discussion will outweigh the negative feelings that may ensue. Two Mental Sign people will tend to have a controlled, rational conversation, busily organizing and sorting out their thoughts about how they both feel.

An Air Sign man with a balanced chart can be the epitome of cooperation and objectivity; Air encompasses the gift of being able to consider people, events, and ideas outside its own realm of experience. Air Sign men tend to be very fair-minded about their perceptions. But after they have reviewed and dissected everything, there may be a very blunt synopsis. They can unwittingly hurt others with their penchant for "honesty at all cost." They are sometimes unnecessarily truthful, blurting out something that could have been presented in a more tactful manner.

If he believes that he has hurt your feelings, an Air Sign man can suffer a great deal of guilt about it. Because Air is very judgmental (resulting from his extreme perfectionism), he judges himself harshly as well. And then, due to his feeling guilty for having hurt you, he may turn his cold Air on you for your being the cause of his guilt!

Eastern Hemisphere Air: Aquarius, Gemini
Less relationship-oriented
Less concerned with the needs of others

Any of the more self-centered aspects of the Element of Air potentially can be magnified in the Eastern Hemisphere. Remember that the Eastern Signs are more focused on themselves and less concerned with your needs. These two Signs are among the most self-centered and controlling of the zodiac. A man with his Sun Sign in the Eastern Hemisphere needs a number of planets in the Western Hemisphere to balance out his self-centered nature. With the right overall chart, either one of these men could be terrific for Air or Earth Sign women.

Western Hemisphere Air Sign: Libra
More relationship-oriented
More concerned with the needs of others

Being in the Western Hemisphere makes Libra the most relationship-minded of the Air Signs—the most gracious and agreeable, the least self-centered. Definitely my favorite of the Air Sign Men. A Libra man with an overall balanced chart can make about the best mate of the zodiac for an Air or Earth Sign woman.

The Gemini Man: Air Thinking Sign
(May 22–June 21)

ELEMENT: Air (an abstract, idealistic brand of thinking).

Independent, Futuristic, Intellectual, Restless, Creative, Humanitarian.

GENDER: Masculine (Martian, confrontive).

EASTERN HEMISPHERE

A MUTABLE SIGN: Flexible and changeable.

Emotionally compatible only with Air and Earth women.

If you are contemplating an involvement with a Gemini man, you really should be an Air Sign woman (Gemini, Libra, Aquarius) who will share his idealistic, curious, analytical nature. Analyzing him, however, may seem futile; the minute you think you have him figured out, surprise! It's Mr. Unpredictable! This man, for whom boredom is a fate worse than death, will either infuriate you with some harebrained idea, or kidnap you from your office and take you on a picnic in the rain. If you think that is a harebrained idea, that is where the trouble could start! This is where the Earth Sign woman (without enough Air in her chart) might decide that this man is not grounded enough for her more practical approach to life. The abstract, analytical Air brand of thinking is very different from Earth's way of operating. It would, therefore, be necessary that a Gemini man have a major planet or two in the Earth Signs if he is to identify with the Earth woman's more practical, down-to-earth nature. This woman would also need to have major planets in Air in order to relate to the impractical dreamer in this man. If you find yourself a Gemini who isn't very restless or changeable, he would undoubtedly have a great deal of Earth and Fixed influence in his chart, which could stabilize the typically fickle Gemini spirit.

When he does manifest the true Gemini nature, the woman in his life had better not have so much Earth in her chart that she is unable to appreciate his Gemini childlike need for endless variety and excitement. Frankly, most women want and need a man who is a good deal more emotionally solid and predictable than the average Gemini man. These men are truly an enigma. He may shower you with love and attention, and then act as though you are bothering him if you call when he is distracted with something else. An Air Sign man is capable of being there for you one minute with his gracious, considerate Air qualities (the soft breeze) and then—presto!—he is aloof and removed the next minute (the arctic chill)! You suddenly feel "emotionally homeless"!

So emotionally erratic, so elusive in his approach to life and love, this man usually cannot offer a woman the sense of stability and the feeling of security that are necessary for a woman to feel protected by the man she loves. This can be especially difficult for women with a more insecure or vulnerable nature, who really need to feel that they can count on a man to be there for them. I would be inclined to recommend a Gemini man only to women who are very emotionally mature and independent. He has such an independent nature and such a need for "alone time" that women who are not emotionally secure could easily feel rejected by him. Add his penchant for changing his mind (perhaps about how he feels about *you*) and his gregarious personality, and you can see how these men could make a very secure woman feel insecure!

Gemini men should be avoided at all cost by Water and Fire Sign women, whose need for emotional interaction makes the extremely sensitive Air Sign men feel anxious. Water and Fire women need profoundly devoted mates, and are not going to feel that kind of everlasting ardor from a Gemini man. He is incapable of expressing passion in a way that will make an Emotional Sign woman really feel it. And a man who can change his mind so readily does not exactly give a woman the feeling of devotion and undying love that Water and Fire women crave. A Feeling Sign woman is searching for an emotional soul mate; he is looking for someone on his mental wavelength. You are more impulsive; he is more rational. He likes to think things through; you like to act on your feelings. A Water Sign woman with emotional insecurities would be the worst mate for a Gemini man.

Another thing to be aware of with Gemini men: when they have too many major planets in the masculine Elements of Air or Fire, they have an overabundance of masculine traits. Men with too much Martian influence can have real problems (see Chapter 5: Why Can't a Man Be More Like a Woman?). They tend to be too opinionated, judgmental, idealistic, impatient, self-centered, and controlling. Control is a particular issue for the Element of Air. A Gemini man often needs to be in total control, not only of his emotions, but of yours as well. He is equally in need of not having anyone else try to control him. When a Gemini man also has an overall high Air imbalance, he can be very touchy. He would tend to misinterpret your need to simply express your feelings as an attempt to control him.

We must also remember that Gemini is located in the Northeastern quadrant of the zodiac, making it among the three most self-centered of all the Signs (Aries and Taurus are the other two). These men are innately focused on their own needs. Of course, there could be a Gemini man with enough major planets in the Western Hemisphere to modify this self-oriented approach to life. Such a man could be absolutely terrific—but for Earth and Air women only!

The Libra Man: Air Thinking Sign
(September 24–October 23)

ELEMENT: Air (an abstract, idealistic brand of thinking).

Independent, Analytical, Artistic, Romantic, Partnership-Minded.

GENDER: Masculine (Martian, confrontive).

WESTERN HEMISPHERE

A CARDINAL SIGN: Energetic and ambitious.

Emotionally compatible only with Air and Earth women.

The Libra man is my first choice of the Air Sign men. These thoughtful, considerate, caring men can make wonderful and loyal mates. Libra is much more relationship-minded, and will be far more interested in meeting your needs, than the other Air Sign men (Aquarius and Gemini). Libra is the only Air Sign in the more relationship-oriented Western Hemisphere. Libra is also the Sign of partnership; people of this Sign have an innate urge to do things with a partner. Being a freedom-oriented Air Sign, they have an independent nature, but there is a basic longing to pair up and approach life and its many challenges and adventures in twos. These gracious, kind, sensitive, creative, artistic, poetic men can make terrific mates for half the women of the zodiac. They are the most agreeable and easygoing of the Air Sign men, and the only Sign I can wholeheartedly recommend to all of the Mental Sign women.

But it seems only fair to warn you about the infamous Libra smile—a big part of their charm! Suddenly you find yourself not caring that he can never make up his mind about anything, is always late, is too idealistic (perhaps overly concerned with what others think), and is sometimes distracted or emotionally distant.

Libra is ruled by Venus, the planet of love and beauty, and therefore has a great appreciation for everything beautiful and symmetrical. Neptune in Libra gave us a generation focused on love and beauty (the "flower children"). Librans are repulsed by anything harsh or crude; they seek balance in their lives and have a great need for harmonious surroundings. Being an idealistic lover of beauty, the more beautiful and tranquil his environment, the happier a Libra man will be. This is not a man who wants to come home to a cluttered house and a kitchen that looks as though it hasn't been thoroughly cleaned since the spring of 1978. This man likes perfection in everything around him. Libra almost outdoes Virgo in this department. The greatest difference is that he is not as likely to do the work himself to have things in order. He may not even say much to you about it. Even though Air is a confrontive Element, unless there are three or more total planets in Air or Fire, Libra can have a problem being confrontive enough. This is due to the fact that he has a tremendous need for peace and harmony. In striving for a gracious, pleasant ambiance in all aspects of his life, he may just sulk privately and deal with the inner stress rather than say anything about it. He needs to present a picture-perfect life to the world. Anything you do to tarnish that image may subtract appreciably from his feelings for you.

Unfortunately, all Air Sign men can have a problem with "overly masculine" behavior. When there are too many planets in the Martian Elements of Air or Fire, it can cause the individual to be exceedingly idealistic, opinionated, assertive, judgmental, and controlling (see Chapter 5: Why Can't a Man Be More Like a Woman?). Fortunately, the Libra man with too many planets in the Air or Fire Signs is not as likely to display these traits in the almost arrogant manner of the other Air Signs who have this problem. He will be more polite and gracious in the way he goes about it; he will smile that smile of his while maneuvering things to his advantage!

I must strongly caution Water and Fire women regarding this Sign; Libra men can readily appear to be on your emotional wavelength. Librans, with their highly sensitive nature and extreme need for a relationship, can be the most deceptive of the Mental Sign men (not that it would be their intention to deceive you). You will feel sure that I must be wrong about Libra being a poor match for you. Actually, they *are* very emotional—in a mental kind of way! Their thoughts are very emotional! Libras are in love with love! They have very romantic souls. But unfortunately, since Libra is a Thinking Sign, it is rarely possible for them to display or express all of this internal emotionality in a manner that is rewarding and fulfilling to a Fire or Water Sign woman with her constant need for emotional connection.

There is a vague, distant quality that Air Sign men possesses, which makes them too emotionally elusive for Emotional Sign women. The Air Sign man's emotions always have to be under control; Emotional Sign women (particularly Fire) want a man who can be out of control once in a while! Fire women also like a man who is capable of self-analysis. They need a man to care about changing and improving a relationship. Oddly enough, though Libra is into analyzing all aspects of everything else, most Libra men do not seem particularly taken by the concept of self-analysis. There are, of course, exceptions to this. A very confident Libran may operate from his Air curiosity, honesty, and objectivity in terms of seeking self-improvement.

Another thing to be aware of with a Libra man: don't expect him to back you up on issues that he hasn't had the time to look at from every angle! He has a hard time being supportive of feelings that he may not be able to personally understand, justify, or rationalize in his mind. Libra has that Air thing about wanting to be fair, though it is not as much of a compulsion as it is with Aquarius. When you combine that trait with his difficulty in making up his mind—well, you may have forgotten the issue before he decides that he is able, in good conscience, to support you!

If you are a Fire Sign woman, this sort of thing can make you want to scream! You need a man to jump in and be there for you, and then dissect the details later if he must. This is one of the reasons why both Fire and Water women, who need to feel unconditional support from a mate, can become frustrated with a Libra man. It's not that you need him to always agree with you or take your side on everything. An Emotional Sign woman just needs to feel a certain protective quality that is missing if a man is busy with all the facts and details instead of offering his immediate emotional support. However, the Mental Sign woman will be able to understand a person giving priority to thoughts and facts. Libra is emotionally compatible with Earth and Air women, but for the Earth woman he ought to have a major planet or two in Earth in order to better relate to her more practical and logical brand of thinking.

The Aquarius Man: Air Thinking Sign (January 21–February 19)

ELEMENT: Air (an abstract, idealistic brand of thinking).

Independent, Futuristic, Intellectual, Restless, Creative, Humanitarian.

GENDER: Masculine (Martian, confrontive).

EASTERN HEMISPHERE

A FIXED SIGN: Determined and persistent.

Emotionally compatible only with Air and Earth women.

The Aquarius man possesses many qualities that may intrigue, charm, and attract you; he is outgoing and candid, has a sweet disposition, and is demonstrative in his affections. The typical Aquarian has an extremely creative mind that works like radar. Many of the Pulitzer and Nobel Prize winners have strong Aquarius influence in their charts—born to challenge and change the world with their humanitarian nature and highly original thinking processes. In fact, the Aquarius man may be so busy saving all of humanity that he somehow forgets about you. But, of course, if he is having a relationship with you in the first place, that must mean that you are also concerned with the human predicament, and that you are probably as independent as he is. He is, indeed, fiercely independent, and may, therefore, assume that you can take care of yourself.

Unlike the fellow Air Sign of Libra, the Aquarius man will not be overly focused on outer beauty; with his appreciation of intellect, he will be more impressed with what is in your head.

Captivate him with your brilliance; he loves a scintillating conversationalist!

Aquarius men are emotionally compatible with their own Element of Air and the other Mental Element of Earth. An Earth woman will be taken by the Aquarian's clever mind and thoughtful nature, but she needs a man to be logical and practical as well. He really should have at least two major planets in the Earth Signs in order to be pragmatic enough for an Earth woman. These Thinking Sign women will appreciate the Air Sign man's caution and his reluctance to jump head-first into a relationship. They need to have the time to dissect and analyze it first. However, when the Air traits of impatience and impulsiveness overrule Air's cautious and fearful side, you may find an Aquarius man who will enter into a relationship without hesitation; invariably this man will have major Fire in his chart.

Though a Fire or Water woman may find an Aquarius man most appealing, with his quick wit and charismatic personality, this man is a definite astrological mismatch for an Emotional Sign woman. He can be wonderfully romantic, not only with the perfect gesture or thoughtful gift, but with his uncanny way of blurting out the right comment at just the right moment to make your heart stand still. But, though he may be sincere, it can all seem like an illusion to an Feeling Sign woman. For you, he will always be emotionally elusive. You will never feel that he really understands your feelings. While a Water Sign woman would feel wounded by his removed attitude, a Fire Sign woman may be infuriated by the Aquarian inability to carry on the kind of emotional interaction that she considers to be daily fare. Both Fire and Water women need a man who can relate to them in a very emotional way—a man who is comfortable talking about how he feels.

The Aquarian man may initially indicate a flat-out lack of interest, possibly to the point where you think he doesn't even like you, much less love you. This gives him time to review your qualities. Aquarians can be very idealistic and perfectionistic when it comes to love—or anything else, for that matter. If you are seriously interested in an Aquarian gentleman (and they usually are gentlemen; they are too refined to be otherwise), you had better be a bit on the shy and elusive side. If you are not intriguing to him, you will never spark his interest. But don't go overboard either; if you get into playing jealousy games, you will lose him altogether.

Incidentally, you can be assured that he will have equal respect for your independence; Aquarians are incredibly fairminded. Also, expect that his friends will be an extremely important part of his life. Aquarius is in the house of friendship. You may tend to feel a bit neglected at times, in that he will not only ignore you to be with his friends, but sometimes to be with strangers. After all, he is out to save the world, and he may have to do it one lost soul at a time!

While all men have the Martian need for appreciation and admiration, those with important planets in the Signs of Aquarius or Leo have a particularly strong need in this regard. The Aquarius man absolutely must believe that he is seen accurately and appreciated; it is imperative to his happiness within a relationship.

And remember, this man needs a great deal of space; all Air Signs need a lot of alone time. Aquarius and Sagittarius are the most independent Signs in the zodiac. We are talking a profoundly freedom-oriented individual! Don't ever forget how incredibly independent the Aquarius man is. If you pressure this guy, his disappearing act could make you think he had joined the Witness Protection Program!

15

All This Applies to Animals, Too

Yes, as long as you know an animal's date of birth, you can apply all of this astrological insight to your lop-eared rabbit or pet iguana!

You will be thrilled to know that there is a logical explanation for why your kitty freaks when you relocate his cat tree. He may be a Taurus; they hate change! His astrological Sign could also explain why your pooch pouts and frets when his dinner is served at odd hours. He might be a Virgo; they look upon unpredictability with great disdain! If he also has a strong Aries influence—they can be so demanding!—he might have attacked you by now!

Looking for a More Affectionate Feline?

Two important chart factors come to mind. Venus and Mercury in the same Sign will give a cat an above average urge to communicate with you, and a majority of planets in the Western Hemisphere produces a need for others. This would make him unlike the typical cat, whose enthusiastic greeting after your six-week absence amounts to a yawn from the top of the refrigerator. By knowing the chart energies, you are able to select a cat who would need your love and attention so much that he would be more inclined to shower you with the attention you have previously known only from the canine world. In the chart of a human, too much Western Hemisphere influence could produce an overly dependent person; while one needn't worry about enrolling a relationship-junkie kitty in a codependency support group, there can be problems when a cat has an excessively high influence in the Western Hemisphere. He can so resent being left alone that he decides to redecorate while you're at work and relocate his bathroom to your closet.

If you have a very powerful and dynamic personality, and you tend to become impatient when you're upset, you would want to avoid a cat with ultrasensitive chart factors, such as having many planets in the two extremely sensitive Elements of Air or Water. This would cause a pet to respond to you with nervousness and anxiety.

Perfect Puppies (Astrologically Speaking)

This information can be extremely helpful in finding the right dog when safety is an issue. For example, a family with a very young child needs a dog whose gentle nature is such that he would never become vicious if a child were to harass him. You would want to avoid a dog with Sun and Mars in the same Sign or a dog with four or more major planets in the Martian Elements of Air and Fire. It is handy that this can all be determined by the chart, saving you unnecessary trips around town looking at litters born on the wrong day.

When discipline is not your forte, it will make your life a great deal easier if you find a puppy whose chart indicates that he has an agreeable and flexible disposition. If you make the mistake of acquiring a puppy with extremely high Fixed influence, this could be the potty-training experience from Hell! One would need to make sure that he learns whatever you intend to teach him, because he'll *never* unlearn it! And you will want enough Venusian influence (probably two major planets) so that the puppy would be more open to doing things your way. A Super-Martian dog would be somewhat less than ideal to train.

Looking for a dog who will be exceptionally affectionate? You will need Venus and Mercury in the same Sign, and the Sun

Sign along with two other major planets in the Western Hemisphere. Too much Western influence can make a dog too obsessed with being near you all the time. Leaving a dog with this imbalance alone is not only upsetting to us because of the way he cries when we leave, but with enough Martian in his chart, you could come home to a house that is no longer standing!

Now, let's look at a true story to see how picking a puppy with the "perfect chart" produces the "perfect dog." For Christmas, I gave my sister a red toy poodle puppy. Her chart is beautifully balanced in all respects (Elements, Hemispheres, Modes, and Gender). Her Martian is a little high, which might have been a problem if she were male. Red Roxy is a Leo with Moon in Aquarius. This confident little dog is exceptionally alert and curious about everything (Venus in Libra). Being the most creative Element (Fire and Air), she has actually figured out that if she puts her ball on a throw rug and then shakes the rug, it will cause the ball to roll so that she can chase it. Roxy loves to go out, but is also fine with staying home (Hemisphere balance). And she is extremely sweet and loving (Mars in Cancer). The effort put into finding a balanced chart rather than picking a puppy based only on its precious face and adorable personality (Roxy has these too) is worth it a thousand times over!

A Horse? Of Course He Must Have the Right Chart

If you're looking for a horse or pony for an inexperienced rider or a child, you will want a very balanced chart. You will also want to make a point of avoiding a horse with no planets in the Water Signs. Water influence is necessary, as it is the "tranquilizer" in a chart. Without Water emphasis, a horse would overreact to stimuli, shying at things that a horse with a balanced chart would hardly notice.

For a show horse, you will definitely want enough Fire for presence. The ideal Element combination for an English show horse who must possess a very dynamic and fiery presence would be the Elements of Fire and Air.

You don't just want a horse, you want a pet! You want your horse to run over to the fence to greet you when you walk up to the paddock! This is not common in horses (they're more like cats), but it can be found. A horse that is this interested in relating to its owner will have at least two factors in his chart: a majority of planets in the Western Hemisphere, and Venus and Mercury in the same Sign. This will make him want to "talk" to you!

How about an endurance horse? High Cardinal (Aries, Cancer, Libra, Capricorn) would be excellent for endurance trials or for any endeavors in which physical stamina is an issue. If Sun, Mars, or Moon were in the Cardinal Signs it would be ideal. Bear in mind that this horse should not be kept in a stall—at least not without getting out every day. Planets in Scorpio or Taurus would also be good to help with drive and determination.

Believe it or not, a chart factor that I have seen contribute to the ability of jumpers is high Air influence. I would like to see some Fire and Cardinal along with it.

Palavering Parrots

What about birds? A balanced chart is very important. Birds are so sensitive by nature that major imbalances which produce ultrasensitivity could make a bird very difficult to tame or handle. Certainly a parrot with the communication planets of Venus and Mercury in the same Sign could develop such an extensive vocabulary that he could mimic all of your key phrases. It could prove embarrassing to have such a verbally skilled birdie!

16

So You're in Love with an Emotional Alien

You love him very much and you believe that he sincerely loves you, even though he doesn't have a clue about who you are emotionally; he knows not from your deepest feelings and needs. But now you know why this is so, after learning about your clashing Sun Signs, and you're really depressed! Well, take heart—there may be hope!

It is sometimes possible for couples with a Thinker-Feeler clash to have an emotionally healthy relationship. It doesn't happen very often. But when it does, it always seems to involve the following factors: they are both very evolved and mature individuals; they are very much in love; and they not only have no significant additional negative chart issues to contend with, but their charts reflect various positive factors in terms of compatibility.

First of all, it is imperative that both parties read and re-read this chapter and Chapter 3, which explains the Thinker-Feeler clash. It is imperative that the Feeler work to understand why the Thinker is more instinctively emotionally reserved, and that the Thinker strive to better appreciate how emotion is virtually the Feeler's lifeline. Each person must have respect for the other's emotional nature. Respect increases the chance that you will treat each other's feelings with the care that is essential in any relationship but of utmost importance when partners are such emotional opposites.

What If Your Mate Refuses to Read This?

If you are in a relationship with someone who refuses to read this information, after you have enthusiastically shared how important it is to you, you probably have problems other than your clashing Signs. Such a person lacks the understanding that emotionally grown-up people do things for which their mate has expressed a great desire whenever it is humanly possible to do so. Emotionally mature people understand that to not do so is selfish and childish, and demonstrates an unfamiliarity with the basic concepts of respect and consideration. Your mate may or may not agree with the information presented, but a flat-out unwillingness to review it should not be accepted nor tolerated. Doing so reflects a lack of respect for oneself.

By the way, be certain that you are asking in the right way. You would be amazed at how even the slightest implication that you are insisting or giving an ultimatum can have a negative effect. Martians are resistant to unsolicited advice and to being "told" what to do! A wonderful communication tool is to officially ask your mate if he would like to hear some thoughts on a particular subject before sharing your pearls of wisdom. Usually, curiosity alone will cause him to say "yes." Remind him that he is free to stop you if the conversation makes him uncomfortable and he would rather finish it at another time. It is amazing how this habit of asking someone if they would like to hear your feelings or thoughts will make them so much more open to hearing them than if you were to deliver the same information without an official green light from him.

Just as being too Martian can be counterproductive, so will it be self-defeating to be too Venusian in requesting what you desire. There is a strong Venusian tendency to be too accepting, too agreeable—not to "expect" things. It is important to blend the Martian and Venusian energies. Make sure that you read Chapter 5: Why Can't a Man Be More Like a Woman? to fully understand how we all need to blend our Martian and Venusian sides in order to be more effective communicators—in order to become "Marusians."

A Thinker will usually resist new input more than a Feeler will, due to the fact that they are less inclined to open up emotional issues in the first place. Earth people will be even more reluctant than Air people, in that they will resist through their Venusian energy as well; Venus seeks peace and harmony.

Learn to Really Listen to Your Partner

My first suggestion to help the Thinker-Feeler couple can also help with stimulating a mate's interest in the project in the first place. An amazing thing happens when we stop and really listen to someone express his or her feelings—listen without judging, advising, or criticizing. This is called "active listening," and it involves making a real project out of the listening process.

A wonderful book by Dr. Thomas Gordon, entitled *Parent Effectiveness Training,* explains this important tool of active listening; it is simply "playing back" to someone what you thought you heard him or her say (or what you perceive he or she may be feeling). You may do this word for word (parroting) or you may restate it in your own words—but don't include any input, criticism, judgment, or advice.

This has to be the single most important communication skill that anyone can use to improve any relationship with anyone. It is so effective that it can transform troubled relationships. Unfortunately, it seems to be a difficult habit to develop—especially for those with high Martian influence. This is because they would rather jump in and start giving advice the minute they hear or think they hear a problem. And, of course, if they think they heard something really stupid or outrageous, they want to satisfy their urge to say so and then jump in with their ideas. This is particularly unfortunate in that the real magic of active listening is that it helps people to sort out or make sense of what they are saying in the first place. If we jump in to criticize, mend, or find a solution, we may be helping them solve the wrong problem. And if they feel in any way judged, not only are they not feeling our unconditional support, but they are not going to want to share their feelings in the future, for fear of being ridiculed or judged.

Make a Commitment to Genuinely Care About the Other's Feelings

Perhaps the single most important thing in a relationship is that the other party really feels our love for them. We must therefore be committed to the concept that what is important is not what *we* perceive to be a satisfactory way of communicating our love, but how our mate perceives our expression of love. One way to explain the contrast in communication style between the Thinker and the Feeler is to say that they have opposite "styles" of communicating their emotions.

An awareness of the "communication style" that your mate needs can be a giant step toward small changes that you can make in order to come closer to meeting his or her needs.

Remember, this is not just a desire on your mate's part, but a real need; this is what your mate needs in order to feel your love and in order to feel that you sincerely care about his or her feelings.

One needs to begin with the premise that the other person is right about how our communication style misses the mark with them. Who else would be the expert on your mate's needs? Surely no one but your mate! We tend to lose sight of this fact when we feel criticized by someone's interpretation of how our current method of communication is lacking for them.

We all have relationships that involve the Thinker-Feeler clash—if not with our mate, then with family members, friends, coworkers, and so on. We must approach these situations with sincere respect for the fact that we are cut from different emotional cloth. Regrettably, we tend to go forth with the fundamental belief that our cloth is better than theirs. While this is human nature, it is an unfortunate position to embrace. Our cloth is not better, only different!

If You Are a Feeler (Water or Fire Sign) and Your Mate Is a Thinker (Earth or Air Sign)

You must remember that as surely as you need—perhaps crave—your brand of emotional connection, the Thinker needs a more reserved or laid back kind of emotional connection. His or her brand of emotional connection may sometimes strike you as more of a "disconnection," particularly if your brand of emotional interaction is very fiery! You need to remember that you are basically "emotional opposites." Just as you will react emotionally and then need to stop and process your thoughts, he or she will do the opposite: thinking about the situation to determine how he or she feels. While you cannot change the basic nature of your Thinking Sign partner, there are ways to help your Thinking partner be more comfortable with expressing emotions.

One important goal is to make your Thinking Sign mate as emotionally comfortable as possible. In extreme cases, a Mental Sign man could be so anti-emotion that the mere thought of a discussion about anything other than "safe" subjects (news and weather, etc.) can make him immediately wary; he tends to assume that talking about feelings will turn into an argument, or at the very least, an emotional discussion.

Be supportive of little efforts he may make to share his feelings with you. Let go of any expectations that you may have as to exactly how he should express himself. Don't take it personally when he is not "there" for you in the way you would prefer. Remember, whatever seems lacking does not reflect a lack of love for you, only a lack of ability to communicate it in a way that would be more emotionally fulfilling to you.

If the Thinker's chart has most of the major planets in Earth and/or Air Signs, and your Feeling chart has strong influences in Water and/or Fire, the difference between your strong desire for emotional interaction and his resistance to it can be very great indeed. This type of chart clash would present an enormous challenge.

In a situation such as this, the more emotionally mature the individuals are in terms of respecting each other's differences, the more potential there is to find a level of compatibility. Specifically, the Thinking Sign person needs to realize that emotion and the expression of it are not such a scary thing, while the Feeling Sign person needs to learn more emotional control and attempt to make important decisions based on the facts in a situation, rather than relying exclusively on their feelings.

If You Are a Thinker (Earth or Air Sign) and Your Mate Is a Feeler (Water or Fire Sign)

If your mate's need for emotional interaction makes you uncomfortable—if he or she complains that you seem distant or removed—there are things that you can do. Though there will always be a difference in the way the two of you approach emotion, it is possible to close the gap a bit.

It is important to let go of the concept that your mate's needs and desires are wrong. It is natural to feel that our way is the right way, and that the other party is from another emotional universe (and, in a way, they are), but take heart; emotional aliens can, in some cases, not only coexist, but find happiness.

The Feeler's need for emotional exchange is as real as your need for emotions to be more controlled and organized. As surely as you may need to think about something before you know for sure how you feel, your mate needs to stop and attempt to sort through feelings to gain more perspective after having reacted emotionally.

If you are an exception, in that you do not always need to have your emotions under control, you probably have two or more major planets in Water or Fire. However, if your sun Sign is in Earth or Air, then, regardless of other chart factors, you will be more cautious and less comfortable overall with feelings and emotional issues than will your more emotionally capricious mate.

The fewer planets a Thinking Sun person has in the Emotional Elements of Water or Fire, the less comfortable he or she is with feelings and interacting in emotional situations. If that describes you, it would be especially difficult for you to understand the highly emotional nature of your mate. If your Feeling Sun mate's chart indicates a lack of major planets in the Mental Elements of Earth and/or Air, it can really add to the emotional gap between you.

In such a situation, the more evolved you and your mate are in terms of respecting differences in one another, the more potential you have to find a level of compatibility. Specifically, the Mental Sign person needs to realize that emotion and the expression of it are not so scary after all, while the Emotional Sign person needs to learn more control over his or her feelings and attempt to make important decisions based on the facts, rather than relying so much on their feelings.

There can be real hope for couples with clashing Signs when both parties are truly committed, not just to an "emotional truce," but to creating an emotionally rewarding relationship. Perhaps the key is the full realization and acceptance of the fundamental differences in emotional makeup. It would be no more realistic for Feelers to expect Thinkers to have the same needs they do than it would for a woman to expect a man to have the needs of a woman.

17

When Parents and Children Have Clashing Signs

What a different world it would be if parents were always astrologically compatible with, and therefore on the same emotional wavelength as, their children!

When the very definition of feeling loved is feeling understood and accepted for who we are, it is tragic that so many parents find it difficult to really understand a child whose emotional makeup differs from their own.

After becoming aware of major incompatibility with a friend or lover, you might choose not to pursue the relationship. This, however, is obviously not an option when it comes to family. And while it is sometimes possible to choose not to associate with a given family member, this is not the case between a parent and a young child. It requires a great deal of time and effort for people to understand their differences and learn to relate to one another in a positive way that allows for the other party being cut from a different emotional cloth.

While understanding your child's emotional nature is extremely important, it becomes critical when his or her approach to emotion is tremendously different from your own. Knowing how crucial this is to the happiness of both child and parent, it seems that bringing a baby home from the hospital without astrological knowledge is like bringing a very valuable plant home from the nursery without any care instructions. In order for it to thrive, do you place it in shade or direct sunlight, and how much water does it require?

There are two areas in particular that can cause a great deal of hurt and misunderstanding when the charts of a parent and child are very dissimilar. The first is, of course, the clash of Sun Signs, and the second is the conflict between Eastern and Western Hemispheres.

The problem that creates the greatest emotional gap between parent and child is the emotional clash between the Thinking and Feeling Signs. Make sure that you have read Chapter 3: The Clash Between Thinkers and Feelers. As you review this chapter, think about the effect that this profound difference in approach to emotionality might have on one's relationship with a child. Please also read Chapter 16: So You're in Love with an Emotional Alien. The information in this chapter can be readily applied to a parent-child relationship.

When the Parent Is a Mental Sign and the Child Is an Emotional Sign

The Thinker-Feeler clash presents more of a problem when the parent is the Thinking Sun Sign and the child is the Feeling Sun Sign. An ultrasensitive Water Sign child, who desperately yearns for emotional responsiveness, could be devastated by a more emotionally reserved Earth Sign parent. This Feeling Sign child is fundamentally comfortable with emotionality and needs a good deal of emotional feedback. Unfortunately, emotional feedback is not second nature to the Thinking Sign parent, who is fundamentally uncomfortable with processing and expressing too much emotion.

As an Earth or Air Sign, who is less comfortable with expressing and coping with emotion, a parent could seem to not understand how the very emotional Water or Fire Sign child really feels. An Aquarian mother could love her Pisces daughter dearly, and be extremely concerned with her needs and desires, but the daughter might have a difficult time feeling that love if her Thinking Sign mother communicates in a manner that seems too cold or removed for her ultrasensitivity.

You may be wondering how your understanding of your different emotional natures can help you make your child feel more loved. This may not be as difficult as you might think; you simply need to alter your approach—your style of communication.

I recommend that you begin by talking with your child about all of this. Tell her that you have new information that you wish to share—knowledge that has helped you to understand that there is a real difference between the two of you in the way that you express love and need to have love expressed to you. Tell her that you are going to make a sincere effort to listen to her needs, and to really hear how she feels. Let her know that you need her help in order to help her—that she needs to tell you when you seem too abrupt or distant or when you talk a manner that makes her uncomfortable. Your child needs to feel that the two of you are a team when it comes to improving your communication with one another.

Here are a few other suggestions that could make all the difference in the world when it comes to making your Feeling Sun Sign child really feel that you are "there" for him or her emotionally:

1. Read *Parent Effectiveness Training,* the excellent book by Dr. Thomas Gordon, and use his important tool of Active Listening. This means simply "playing back" to others what you thought you heard them say or what you perceive they may be feeling. You may do this either word for word (parroting) or paraphrased in your own words—and without any other input, criticism, judgment, or advice. This valuable tool will make your child feel that you are genuinely interested simply because she will really feel heard, without criticism.

This has to be the single most important communication skill that anyone can use in improving any relationship. It is so phenomenally effective that it can totally change a relationship.

2. Take enough time! Just giving a child the feeling that you will make time for him or her is of crucial importance. If it is an

important issue, make sure that when you discuss it you not only have plenty of time for each of you to say what you need to say, but that you are also both in the right frame of mind. If it is a small problem, and will only take a minute, take an extra moment or two just to make your child feel more important than all of the other things in your busy day. Pour a glass of lemonade and sit down to talk. It will not take more than a few extra minutes, and it will make your child feel he or she is important to you.

3. Be very aware of the tone of your voice. Emotional Sign children, especially Water Sign children, need to be talked to in a pleasant tone of voice with a calm manner. Their sensitivity is such that a harsh attitude, or one which they perceive as such, can crush them deeply. If you are an Earth Sign (Capricorn or Taurus; this is not as true with Virgo) your child may see your demeanor as so practical and down to earth that you come across as too cold or uncaring. If you are an Air Sign (Gemini, Libra, or Aquarius) your Emotional Sun Sign child might view your manner as aloof. The bottom line for either an Earth or Air Sign parent who needs to communicate with more warmth and expression of positive feeling is to add a more gentle, loving tone to your voice and to your style of communication when dealing with these ultrasensitive children.

4. Talk about how you *feel* rather than what you think. These children operate instinctively from their emotions, basing everything on how they feel. When trying to communicate with a mother or father whose Sign is Mental, they often become frustrated because that parent is speaking a different language when it comes to talking about feelings. If you are an Earth or Air Sign parent, you will be inclined to talk about your thoughts rather than your feelings, using words and phrases that reflect that tendency. For instance, you might want to say, "I think that we need to remember . . ." But the Emotional Sign child would relate better to, "I feel that we need to remember . . ." This may seem like a silly thing, but it is amazing how much difference a change of one word can create. Along the same line, when asking someone to do something, a gentler

approach is to use the words "will" or "would," rather than "can" or "could." Try, "Will you please pick up your clothes?" rather than, "Can you please pick up your clothes?" The person being asked knows that he or she *can* do it; it's just a question of whether he or she *chooses* to. Therefore, using "will" or "would" seems to be providing the opportunity to process it and arrive at a conclusion (empowering the child), rather than perceiving the situation in terms of being coerced or manipulated. It may seem subtle, but it is very powerful.

5. Occasionally, give feelings priority over facts, and think about how your child feels. It is common for an Earth or Air Sign parent to look at the situation in terms of the facts when making decisions, instead of letting the child's feelings and emotional needs be the guideline. For example, allowing a child to stay up past bedtime to visit with a favorite uncle who will be away for six months would be putting the child's emotional needs first. A Mental Sign parent's first thoughts on the subject may be about the child's missed sleep. The focus would tend to be on the fact that a child needs a certain number of hours of sleep every night in order to be physically healthy. However, a child has emotional needs that must be met in order to be mentally and emotionally healthy.

When the Parent Is an Emotional Sign and the Child Is a Mental Sign

It is extremely important that, as a Fire or Water Sign parent, you understand that your Earth or Air Sign child does not share your comfort zone in dealing with emotion. You could make a tremendous difference in your child's future, in terms of how he or she will process emotion throughout life. Your child needs to learn that emotion is not such a scary thing. There are probably many more emotionally disturbed people with Mental Sun Signs than there are with Emotional Sun Signs, because the Mental Sign people find it so much more difficult to cope with their feelings (whether they be feelings of anger, depression, disappointment, or frustration).

You can help your Mental Sign child to understand that, while this fear of feelings is part of his or her nature, there really is nothing to be afraid of—that all emotions are a normal part of everyone's life. Encourage the child to learn to accept emotion, to express feelings no matter what they are. Help your child to understand how vital this is to emotional health, and that the fear of feeling is more frightening than the feeling itself. Refer to Chapter 7: Is He an Emotional Grownup? Pay particular attention to the explanation of the importance of expressing anger, and to the material on ego states. Unexpressed anger has to be the number-one cause of emotionally related mental and physical illnesses. Remember, it is far better that a child express anger too strongly than not at all.

Because this child is so uncomfortable with too much emotional intensity, you must be very careful in the way you communicate with him or her. It is profoundly negative for a parent to berate or scream at a Mental Sign child. Air Sign children are especially sensitive to emotional upheaval. They can become physically sick when confronted with emotional trauma.

When a Child Is Astrologically More Needy and More Giving Than the Parent

The other astrological factor that can present major areas of misunderstanding between parent and child involves an imbalance of Hemisphere influence between the two charts. There is an enormous difference between individuals with very strong Western Hemisphere influence and those with strong Eastern Hemisphere influence. When this imbalance exists between parents and children, it would have the greatest potential negative effect when the parent is strongly Eastern Hemisphere and the child has major emphasis in the Western Hemisphere.

The most pronounced difference between these Hemispheres is that Eastern people are much more independent, less needy of others and their approval, and fundamentally more self-oriented. Western people are much more needy of close relationships, and more prone to insecurity and rejection. One can easily see how a child with the problems posed by too much Western influence could feel unloved or feel rejected by a parent who has the opposite orientation in regard to this basic issue of needing others. It is not that Eastern people don't love and need other people in their lives; it is a matter of the level and degree of that need. Either imbalance can cause major difficulties. The ideal situation would be to have the major planets evenly distributed between these two Hemispheres. This would allow one to have a strong sense of independence, and a healthy level of need and concern for others.

Incidentally, the Eastern Hemisphere parent can't expect to change and become more organically needy of the type of interaction the Western person craves. This would be as unlikely as the Western individual suddenly no longer needing the kind of bonding and relating with others that is his or her very nature. It is, however, important to truly understand this tremendous difference between you and your child, and attempt to relate to the child accordingly.

By taking the time, making the effort, and thinking of things that you might do or say to make your child feel that you are involved in your relationship in a dynamic way, you can work to offset the differences every day.

If you find yourself automatically saying "no" to your child, stop and re-evaluate the situation. See if there is a possibility that you respond too quickly out of habit. Maybe by putting yourself out just a little more, you might be able to say "yes." Be more open to setting your own needs aside on a given occasion. Unfortunately, some people who are highly Eastern literally do not grasp what that concept is all about. Yes, I know that, as a parent, you have set aside your needs just a few times already. But be honest: have you done it enough lately? Have you done the kinds of things that you know in your heart would really thrill your son or daughter and really make him or her feel special? It can take very little extra effort to drastically improve a relationship that is filled with problems that seem insurmountable.

Please reread Chapter 9: Is He a Natural-Born Couch Potato? This chapter includes important information for every parent. It explains how those with imbalanced Modes (Cardinal, Fixed, Mutable) in their charts can have problems in terms of how they approach projects and situations on a daily basis. Understand the astrological influences that can cause a child to constantly pursue new projects while never completing them, or to be exceedingly stubborn. Most important, look for "notes to parents" throughout the chapter that will be helpful in working with children who have these types of chart imbalances. There is much that can be accomplished during childhood, when the habits of a lifetime are being formed.

18

Somewhere Out There

Since I am full of advice about how to avoid Mr. Wrong, you may be wondering if I have any thoughts on how to go about finding Mr. Right! Fortunately, I have a wonderful suggestion as to how you can simplify the search. My Venus and Mercury in Capricorn produce a very logical approach to this rather bleak task.

Using Personal Ads

For openers, if you abide by the Thinker-Feeler clash theory, you will eliminate half the men of the zodiac. You'd better have a way of meeting a lot of men so that you can sort through them astrologically. I highly recommend that all of my single clients use the personals ads as a way of finding someone who is emotionally compatible.

If you had something of value to sell, such as a car, you would not just tell your friends and put cards up at the supermarket, and then call the junk yard if no one seemed interested. You would advertise it in the newspaper so that someone looking for just such an automobile would find it under the make and year of interest and then call you. Do you see the parallel here? You are something of value! If you have not managed to meet someone at the supermarket, and you have run out of friends with single friends, you do not jump off a cliff!

The classified ads are designed to bring together a person looking for something with a person who has it!

Singles trying to meet singles has been called the greatest social problem of our time. Unfortunately, a few years ago when the personals ads were becoming popular as a way for singles to meet, people became so frightened about the AIDS crisis that many were paranoid about meeting anyone who was not a close friend of a friend. Now most people have come to realize that anyone could have AIDS, and that it is a matter of being responsible enough to practice "safe sex."

Welcome to high-tech dating! Now you get a voice mail box when you place a personals ad, you pick up your messages at your convenience, and you have the advantage of hearing what your respondents sound like. I have clients who tell me that they have never had such a great time meeting men. Some who had exceptionally well-written ads have gotten phenomenal responses—several hundred per month! What fun they had just coming home to ten calls a day. And those singles who are serious about meeting the right mate usually choose to meet people through placing ads as well as answering them.

Incidentally, you may prefer to receive only written responses. You can get important insights from seeing how a man expresses himself in a letter; you know you are in trouble if he has a problem putting sentences together! You may only talk to or meet one out of 40 respondents, wading through hundreds of calls or letters. So what? How else can you have access to such a volume of men (and charts) from which to choose? It will be time-consuming, but the time will have been well spent when you find a wonderful man.

You would be surprised how much fun it can be! Granted, there are vast numbers of Mr. Wrongs out there for every Mr. Right. But nothing ventured, nothing gained. And just think how many funny stories you will have to share with your friends.

And don't give me this nonsense that only desperate women would resort to placing an ad to meet a man. Where have you been lately? This is a very acceptable thing these days. Besides, what's wrong with being eager to be happy, to find a person to share your life with, to become emotionally fulfilled? Anyone who thinks that the personals ads are not a terrific way to meet people is either unfamiliar with the process or exceedingly idealistic. These individuals probably have Mercury (the brain of the chart) in the idealistic element of Fire. They tend to feel that it is too cold and calculating to set a goal to find a man, to approach love in such an "organized" way. Meeting someone has to be "romantic." Maybe not! Webster's dictionary gives one definition of romantic as "impractical in conception or plan." By that definition, having no plan might just be a bit too romantic! It certainly strikes me as impractical to have no plan of action—to just let things happen to you, instead of making things happen.

Some people think that fate should bring two people together. Okay, how about letting fate bring you together through an advertisement? You are simply being realistic enough about how difficult it is for people to find each other, and smart enough to do something about it. You are aware of how wonderful you are and you know how many men you will have to meet in order to find one who deserves you. If you think about it, you needn't be embarrassed about placing ads to meet someone. I would think very positively of a man who would be realistic and organized enough to use this method to meet the right woman, rather than relying on social gatherings and accidental meetings. It also indicates that he has something better to do with his time than frequent singles bars!

Doesn't it make a lot more sense to have a realistic approach to meeting someone than to just sit back thinking that somehow, someday the right man is going to magically cross your path with no effort on your part? This could happen, but you could waste some precious years waiting for it to happen! If you had the desire or goal to find the right anything—from an exercise coach to a therapist—to enhance your life, I doubt that you would stand by waiting for this individual to find you.

Sorting Through the Candidates

Okay, you're now convinced that ads are a terrific way to meet men; how do you tell the crazies from the serious candidates? First, let's focus for a moment on how to determine whether a man has problems. Women are often concerned about having some "disturbed" individual answer their ad. This really is not a problem; by the time you conduct an adequate "phone interview" and acquire his chart information, you should feel comfortable about getting together in a public place.

Naturally, you will ask for his exact date of birth in the outgoing phone message that he will hear if he responds to your ad by phone. While most men are happy to comply, any man who won't give you this information has a "control issue"; he only wishes to give you information that he thinks you need. This shows a lack of respect for what is important to someone else. If he gives you his birth date, you will be able to determine his Sun Sign and know whether he qualifies in terms of the Thinker-Feeler clash.

After you have determined that he is "A.D." (Astrologically Desirable), I recommend lengthy phone interviews to minimize wasted time. You would be amazed at how much insight you can gain by asking the right questions in a telephone conversation. You should always be able to come away with a sense of the whether this man is basically "together." If you are really playing detective, there is much you can learn. You should, in one or two phone encounters, be able to really feel it if this man qualifies on the most fundamental level.

Creating Your List of Mandatory Qualities in a Mate

There is a wonderful way to determine what qualities and traits you must have in a man, as opposed to the ones you would love to have but could live without. I suggest to all of my single clients that they make a Mandatory List that outlines the qualities an individual absolutely must possess before you would even consider him as a life partner (and, therefore, as a date). By the way, some of you tend to consider almost any man who is crazy about you after two dates as a potential mate. I strongly advise you not to even have coffee with a man who doesn't meet the requirements on your Mandatory List.

Each woman's list will be different, but any potential mate or date must have high self-esteem and be considerate, flexible, reasonable, and generous.

In order to help you make your list more accurate, I have found that two things are important. First, you should continue to go back to the drawing board over a period of time to constantly update and upgrade your list. A list that is really right for you will require a great deal of soul searching and evaluation. This is not something you will do in one day, or even in one weekend. You may make a list in a few minutes, but revising this list should be an ongoing process.

Second, it is crucial that you draw a line at the bottom of your list and add a few items under the heading Strongly Preferred. These might include some of the following: athletic, witty, impulsive, organized, and so on. Use a pencil with an eraser. You will probably wrestle with some of these issues, first putting something on your Mandatory List, then realizing that maybe you could live without it if you had to, then saying to yourself, "No, I cannot spend my life with a man who doesn't share my love of children!"

I cannot suggest strongly enough that you make such a list and that you urge all of the unattached people you know to do the same. Even people who are currently in an unhappy relationship might benefit from creating such a list; they might see just how far off base they are with their current mates! It could help them to evaluate whether they ought to remain in the relationship and work on it, or whether it is really hopeless.

It is imperative that you determine in advance what you must have in a mate and what you could do without. Hopefully, you will ultimately learn enough about astrological compatibility factors to include some of these on your list! The most important astrological factor, as you know by now, is the Thinker-Feeler clash.

Getting to Know a Potential Mate

The real test of patience and willpower begins when you find a man who is astrologically suitable and who possesses all of the qualities on your Mandatory List. It can take real willpower to keep from jumping in too quickly. There may be a lurking feeling that if you don't grab him instantly, someone else will. But moving too quickly might be the biggest mistake you could make.

It is essential that two people get to know each other before deciding that they love each other and want to spend eternity together. Beware of the phenomenon known as "courtship behavior." Even people who are exceptionally open, direct, and confrontive indulge in this little ritual when first meeting someone in whom they are very interested. I am not referring to the type of courtship behavior that is used as a mask to cover a dysfunctional personality; I'm talking about the positive version. Everyone puts their best foot forward in the early stages of an exciting relationship. They naturally want to be seen in a positive light, and are trying to impress the other party. Not only is there nothing wrong with this, but there can be everything right about it. During the early stages of any relationship (not just romantic ones), there is an enormous opportunity for two people to bring out the best in each another and to give each other crucial feedback about each other's relating skills.

In Chapter 10, I provide a definition of emotional intimacy. Since emotionally healthy relationships are based on a couple's capacity for emotional intimacy, it is worth repeating the essence of this process. Emotional intimacy is based on both parties making their likes and dislikes known, and both making every attempt, within reason (obviously never achieving anything close to 100 percent) to do less of what the other does not like and more of what the other likes. The degree to which they succeed in listening and adapting in this way determines the exact level and quality of emotional intimacy that any two individuals are capable of achieving.

One of the main reasons why this attention to the genuine needs of one's mate creates such emotional bonding is that it shows the other person that we sincerely care about their needs, even when we cannot meet them. It is crucial to discuss in detail the needs we cannot meet so that our mate feels our concern and understands why we don't believe it's realistic or possible for us to do so. It would often be appropriate to say how sorry we are for being unable to do the thing in question, since we know that it is of real importance.

The initial stage of a relationship is the time when people are the most gracious and the most respectful of each other. This is the all-important time prior to succumbing to something very human: the later stage when you begin to take the other person for granted! This will take place very quickly if you make a decision to become "exclusive" too soon—or, heaven forbid, to move in together too quickly. By putting the cart before the horse and becoming too intimate when you are really only "intimate strangers," you are really asking for trouble. Suddenly, both of you are expecting too much, asking too much of each other before you each have the feeling that the other has the "right" to do so. You begin to feel like, "Who is this person to ask this of me, when I barely know him or her?" We balk about being expected to alter our lifestyle and actions for someone we've just met, no matter how attracted we are or how interested we may be in a meaningful relationship. There are many things that we would be quite happy to do for someone once we have had the chance to develop a sincere feeling of affection, but not before.

Getting Onto the
Communication Highway

There needs to be an opportunity for each party to learn about the other's style of communication—to enter what I call the "communication highway," which must include "rest stops" and "emergency lanes." There isn't a person in this world, no matter how evolved, who will not at times manifest irritating or annoying habits or react to something in a way that is not comfortable for another person. Couples desperately need to have time and space while they discover the bumps in their communication highway. When these unexpected obstacles are encountered, they need to be put in perspective; they can be dealt with much more productively when there is time apart to review a misunderstanding and perceive the situation with greater objectivity. This is impossible if you are spending every spare moment together before you have found positive ways to communicate with each other.

How does your potential mate deal with anger, frustration, disappointment, and stress? At the very least, you must experience how a man copes with these basic emotional issues before you consider your relationship to be past the embryonic stage. You may be extremely excited about the potential for this relationship, but that is indeed all that you can logically be excited about: where it *could* go. You can only find out where it *will* go as time goes by. Please don't assume that this man is something he may not be; don't "build a soul behind a pair of eyes"!

I can hear some of you saying, "But I absolutely know and feel in my soul that this is the person for me, and we just can't stand to be apart, so we can see each other every day and it couldn't possibly be a problem." Wrong! Ironically, the more certain you are that this is the relationship of your life, the more you owe it to yourself and each other to do everything within your power to protect that potential—to respect the great possibilities that lie before you. You need to be as certain as possible that you are not going to allow the little negatives that come up to ruin the feelings between you when they are in that fragile early stage of development. This is a time when you both need your interaction to be of a very positive nature while you are "falling in love." When couples have to cope with too much negative interaction prior to having enough positive emotional history, they simply do not have the emotional foundation that they need in order to handle the problem areas in a healthy manner.

Once you have traveled a distance on that communication highway, and you have come to respect and trust each other in many important ways, only then are you past the "intimate stranger" stage. You have now managed to develop genuine feelings of intimacy and affection. Otherwise, a couple can be so wrapped up in their attraction to each other and the romantic bliss of their best presentation of themselves that, when they hit a bump in the highway, they can end up head-first on the pavement. Having enough time apart early in a relationship is the equivalent of wearing your "romantic seat belt."

Spending time apart gives you time to miss each other, time to wish that you were together, instead of being together so much that you find yourself wishing for time apart! It can be confusing to feel crazy about a person on the one hand, and yet want time apart on the other hand. You might start to wonder just what your feelings are for this person. Even if you think you can handle that feeling, do you want him to feel that about you? Of course you don't; you want him to have time to miss you and time to think about wanting to be with you! I have a theory that this is even more important for a man—part of the process of a man falling in love. Women are basically more relationship-oriented and more into love and romance than men to begin with. A woman seems to naturally possess a greater feeling of urgency about love and to think more about the man when she is away from him even for a short time. Because men don't usually spend as much time yearning for or daydreaming about us, they need that time apart even more so that they develop those feelings.

Men are just a little slower on the romantic uptake, and sometimes need to be hit over the head. They need time to notice that they have profound feelings for you. Time away from you will simply speed up that process! And then there is another obvious benefit: men like a challenge, even if they don't know it. Always being available to him doesn't exactly create any kind of challenge. It does, however, create something you do not want: the taking-you-for-granted syndrome. The worst part of that syndrome is that if he feels he "has" you, that you are "his," he begins in many subtle ways to treat you with less respect, to value you just a little less. Men really need to go through the courting process—to win you!

Again, I urge you to take things slowly. You can't know, when you've just met a man, whether there are some "personality skeletons" in his closet or, worse yet, a major dysfunctional factor that he is adept at concealing. In today's world, it's only common sense to be as cautious as possible, to feel that you truly know a person before you put yourself in a position of possible danger—physical or emotional.

19

The Beginning!

While this is the end of this book, it can be the beginning of a new life for you—a life without the agony of emotionally unfulfilling relationships! But in order to achieve this glorious state, there is a small price that you must pay.

This involves a little self-discipline and restraint on your part. It will mean resisting that great-looking charmer who just moved in downstairs. You know he is about to ask you out, and you also know that you are a Leo and he is an Aquarius, and he is therefore astrologically disastrous for you. Delightful as it is to chat with him in the elevator—I know, he is intelligent, witty, gracious, and charming—you are a Fire Sign and he is an Air Sign, and you are cut of entirely different emotional cloth.

From time to time, you may need to review Chapter 3: The Clash Between Thinkers and Feelers as a reminder of why certain Signs are on another emotional planet. A man's personality may have nothing to do with his true emotional nature. He could be wonderful until he becomes stressed by your fiery Leo personality!

And remember that if a man seems to show an alarming disinterest in your needs; it might be time to review Chapter 8: Men Who Are Hopelessly Self-Centered. This will refresh your memory regarding men with too many planets in the Eastern Hemisphere—men who tend to be a bit preoccupied with their own needs.

And regardless of a man's chart, he must prove himself to be not only among the sane, but among the emotionally mature! If he has not managed to achieve an adult level of emotional functioning prior to your meeting, he is not likely to do so in the near future (see Chapter 7: Is He an Emotional Grownup?).

Finally, don't ever settle for a man who doesn't see you accurately for who you are. If a man ever tells you that he cares about you so much that he is willing to overlook three things about you, you may want to thank him very much for his loving, flexible approach as you inform him that those are your three *best* qualities!

Remember, somewhere out there is a Mr. Right Chart who is looking for your chart energies and therefore looking for you!

Recommended Reading

Gilligan, Carol. *In a Different Voice*. Cambridge: Harvard Press, 1982.

Goleman, Daniel. *Emotional Intelligence*. New York: Bantam Books, 1995.

Gordon, Thomas. *Parent Effectiveness Training*. New York: Penguin Books, 1970.

Gray, John. *Men Are from Mars, Women Are from Venus*. New York: HarperCollins, 1995.

Gray, John. *Mars and Venus in the Bedroom*. New York: Harper-Collins, 1995.

Harris, Thomas A. *I'm Okay, You're Okay*. New York: Avon Books, 1967.

Hayden, Naura. *How to Satisfy a Woman Every Time*. New York: Bibli O'Phile Publishing Company, 1982.

Levant, Ronald. *Between Father and Child*. New York: Penguin Books, 1989.

Nelson, Gerald E. *The One Minute Scolding*. Boulder: Shambhala Publications, Inc., 1984.

Norwood, Robin. *Women Who Love Too Much*. Simon & Schuster, 1985.

About the Author

Amy Keehn is an astrological therapist who specializes in emotional compatibility and has focused for more than a decade on couple counseling. A compelling lecturer, she conducts seminars and workshops throughout California and helps people better understand their emotional natures and relationships. Besides providing astrologically incompatible couples with important insight into their conflicting emotional needs, Ms. Keehn helps many single clients recognize their relationship needs and the chart factors that produce the qualities they must have in a mate.

Amy Keehn, a Sagittarius, lives and practices in San Diego, California. She owns an American Saddlebred horse, Sergius–an Aries, an Amazon parrot, Zoe–a Cancer, and Jillian–a feline without astrological credentials. However, Jillian's somewhat pushy personality leads Ms. Keehn to believe that she has a rather Martian chart. Prior to relocating to San Diego, Ms. Keehn appeared regularly as a guest on a cable television show in Santa Barbara.

If you wish to participate in astrological research or would like a chart or relationship evaluation, call 1-800-990-9188.